Plant Based Recipes for 54 Healthy Cupcakes, with Frosting and Decoration Inspiration

Timmy Icca

This Book belongs

Thanks ever so much to each of my cherished readers for investing the time to read this book!

I know you could have picked from many other books, but you chose this one. So, a big thanks for reading all the way to the end. If you enjoyed this book or received value from it, I'd like to ask you for a favor. Please take a few minutes to **post an honest and heartfelt review on** Amazon.com. Your support does make a difference and helps to benefit other people.

Thanks!

Table of Contents

"The E
beloved
These
people

One
vers
ther
flav
vel
yo
oc
w

Summary

verlasting Appeal of Cupcakes: Cupcakes have been a treat for generations, and their appeal seems to be everlasting. miniature cakes have captured the hearts and taste buds of all over the world, and it's not hard to see why.

of the main reasons cupcakes have such enduring appeal is their tility. With countless flavors, fillings, and frostings to choose from, is a cupcake to suit every palate. Whether you prefer classic rs like vanilla or chocolate, or more adventurous options like red et or salted caramel, there is a cupcake out there that will satisfy r cravings. Additionally, cupcakes can be customized to fit any casion or theme, making them the perfect dessert for birthdays, ddings, or any other celebration.

Another factor contributing to the everlasting appeal of cupcakes is their convenient size. Unlike a traditional cake, which requires slicing and serving, cupcakes are individually portioned and ready to eat. This makes them ideal for parties or events where guests can simply grab a cupcake and enjoy. The small size also allows for easy transport, making cupcakes a popular choice for bake sales or as gifts.

Furthermore, cupcakes have a nostalgic charm that resonates with people of all ages. Many of us have fond memories of baking cupcakes with our grandparents or enjoying them at school parties. The sight of a beautifully decorated cupcake can evoke feelings of joy and nostalgia, reminding us of simpler times. This emotional connection to cupcakes adds to their enduring appeal and makes them a comforting and familiar treat.

In recent years, cupcakes have also benefited from the rise of food trends and social media. The popularity of baking shows and competitions has sparked a renewed interest in cupcakes, with bakers experimenting with unique flavors and intricate designs. Social media platforms like Instagram have allowed these creations to be shared and admired by a wider audience, further fueling the cupcake craze. The visually appealing nature of cupcakes makes them perfect for capturing attention and generating excitement online.

Lastly, cupcakes offer a sense of indulgence and decadence that is hard to resist. The combination of moist cake, creamy frosting, and sometimes even a surprise filling, creates a truly indulgent dessert experience. Cupcakes are often seen as a special treat, reserved for celebrations or moments of self-care. This perception of cupcakes as a luxurious indulgence adds to their appeal and makes them a sought-after dessert option.

In conclusion, the everlasting appeal of cupcakes can be attributed to their versatility, convenient size, nostalgic charm, connection to food trends and social media, and their".

"Celebrating Variety in Cupcake Creations: In today's world, cupcakes have become more than just a sweet treat. They have evolved into a form of art, a way for bakers to express their creativity and celebrate the variety of flavors and designs. Cupcake creations have taken the culinary world by storm, captivating both young and old with their delectable taste and visually stunning appearances.

Gone are the days when a simple vanilla or chocolate cupcake would suffice. Now, bakers are pushing the boundaries of flavor combinations, experimenting with unique ingredients and techniques to create cupcakes that are truly one-of-a-kind. From salted caramel to matcha green tea, the options are endless, allowing individuals to find a cupcake that suits their personal taste preferences.

But it's not just the flavors that have become diverse; the designs of cupcakes have also become increasingly intricate and imaginative. Bakers are using fondant, buttercream, and other decorative elements to transform cupcakes into miniature works of art. From delicate floral designs to whimsical characters, cupcakes have become a canvas for bakers to showcase their artistic talents.

The celebration of variety in cupcake creations goes beyond just the flavors and designs. It extends to the inclusivity and accessibility of cupcakes as well. With the rise of dietary restrictions and preferences, bakers have adapted their recipes to cater to a wide range of needs. Gluten-free, vegan, and allergen-friendly cupcakes are now readily available, ensuring that everyone can indulge in the joy of cupcakes.

Furthermore, the celebration of variety in cupcake creations has also fostered a sense of community among bakers and cupcake enthusiasts.

Cupcake competitions and festivals have become popular events, bringing together individuals who share a passion for these delectable treats. These events provide a platform for bakers to showcase their skills, exchange ideas, and inspire one another to push the boundaries of cupcake creativity even further.

In conclusion, the celebration of variety in cupcake creations has transformed cupcakes from a simple dessert into a form of art. Bakers are constantly pushing the boundaries of flavors and designs, creating cupcakes that are not only delicious but visually stunning as well. The inclusivity and accessibility of cupcakes have also played a significant role in this celebration, ensuring that everyone can enjoy these delectable treats. Cupcake competitions and festivals have further fostered a sense of community among bakers and cupcake enthusiasts, inspiring creativity and innovation in this ever-evolving culinary art form. So, the next time you bite into a cupcake."

"Purpose and Structure of Cupcakes Book: The purpose of the Cupcakes Book is to provide readers with a comprehensive guide to baking and decorating cupcakes. This book aims to inspire both novice and experienced bakers to create delicious and visually appealing cupcakes for various occasions.

The structure of the Cupcakes Book is carefully designed to ensure that readers can easily follow the recipes and instructions. The book is divided into several sections, each focusing on a specific aspect of cupcake baking and decorating.

The first section of the book introduces the basics of cupcake baking, including essential ingredients, equipment, and techniques. This section provides a solid foundation for readers who are new to baking, ensuring that they have a good understanding of the fundamentals before moving on to more advanced recipes.

The subsequent sections of the book delve into different flavor profiles and themes for cupcakes. Each section features a variety of recipes that showcase different flavors, such as chocolate, vanilla, fruit, and even savory options. These recipes are accompanied by detailed step-by-step instructions, ensuring that readers can recreate the cupcakes with ease.

In addition to the recipes, the Cupcakes Book also includes a section on cupcake decorating. This section provides readers with tips and techniques for creating stunning designs using various frosting and piping techniques. From simple swirls to intricate designs, this section aims to empower readers to unleash their creativity and elevate their cupcakes to a whole new level.

To further enhance the learning experience, the Cupcakes Book also includes vibrant and enticing photographs of the finished cupcakes. These visuals serve as a source of inspiration and help readers visualize the end result they can achieve with each recipe.

Furthermore, the Cupcakes Book incorporates helpful tips and troubleshooting advice throughout its pages. These tips address common challenges that bakers may encounter, such as achieving the perfect texture, preventing cupcakes from sinking, and troubleshooting frosting issues. By providing these insights, the book aims to empower readers to overcome any obstacles they may face and achieve bakery-quality cupcakes every time.

Overall, the Cupcakes Book is a comprehensive and user-friendly guide that combines delicious recipes, detailed instructions, inspiring visuals, and helpful tips. Whether you are a beginner or an experienced baker, this book is designed to help you master the art of baking and decorating cupcakes, and create delectable treats that will impress your friends and family."

"How to Use This Guide to Cupcake Mastery of Cupcakes: Welcome to the ultimate guide to cupcake mastery! Whether you're a beginner or an experienced baker, this guide will provide you with all the information and tips you need to create delicious and beautiful cupcakes that will impress everyone.

To make the most of this guide, it's important to follow the steps and instructions carefully. Let's dive into the different sections and explore how you can use this guide to become a cupcake master.

1. Understanding the Basics:

In this section, we will cover the fundamental aspects of cupcake baking. From the ingredients you'll need to the equipment required, we'll provide you with a comprehensive overview. Make sure to read this section thoroughly to ensure you have everything you need before you start baking.

2. Mastering the Cupcake Batter:

The key to a perfect cupcake lies in the batter. In this section, we'll guide you through the process of creating a flawless cupcake batter. We'll discuss the importance of measuring ingredients accurately, the different mixing techniques, and how to achieve the ideal consistency. By following our tips and tricks, you'll be able to create cupcakes with a light and fluffy texture every time.

3. Exploring Flavor Combinations:

Cupcakes are not just about the base batter; they're also about the delicious flavors you can infuse into them. In this section, we'll provide you with a variety of flavor combinations that will take your cupcakes to the next level. From classic vanilla and chocolate to more adventurous options like salted caramel or lemon raspberry, you'll find something to suit every taste.

4. Perfecting the Frosting:

No cupcake is complete without a delectable frosting. In this section, we'll guide you through the process of creating different types of frostings, including buttercream, cream cheese, and ganache. We'll also share tips on how to achieve the perfect piping consistency and decorate your cupcakes like a pro.

5. Decorating Techniques:

If you want to take your cupcakes from ordinary to extraordinary, this section is for you. We'll introduce you to various decorating techniques, such as piping flowers, creating intricate designs, and using edible decorations. With our step-by-step instructions and visual examples, you'll be able to create stunning cupcakes that will wow your friends and family.

6. Troubleshooting and Tips:

Even the most experienced bakers encounter challenges from time to time. In this section, we'll address common cupcake baking issues and provide you with troubleshooting tips."

"Understanding the Basics of Cupcake Baking: Cupcake baking is a popular and enjoyable activity that allows individuals to create delicious and visually appealing treats. Whether you are a beginner or an experienced baker, understanding the basics of cupcake baking is essential for achieving successful results.

The first step in cupcake baking is gathering the necessary ingredients. The basic ingredients for cupcakes include flour, sugar, butter, eggs, milk, baking powder, and vanilla extract. It is important to use high-quality ingredients to ensure the best flavor and texture in your cupcakes.

Once you have gathered your ingredients, the next step is to preheat your oven to the appropriate temperature. Most cupcake recipes call for a temperature of around 350 degrees Fahrenheit (175 degrees Celsius). Preheating the oven ensures that your cupcakes bake evenly and rise properly.

Next, you will need to prepare your cupcake pans. This can be done by lining the pans with cupcake liners or greasing them with butter or cooking spray. Cupcake liners not only make it easier to remove the cupcakes from the pan but also add a decorative touch to your finished product.

Now it's time to mix your cupcake batter. In a large mixing bowl, combine the dry ingredients (flour, sugar, and baking powder) and whisk them together to remove any lumps. In a separate bowl, cream together the butter and sugar until light and fluffy. Then, add the eggs one at a time, mixing well after each addition. Finally, alternate adding the dry ingredients and the milk to the butter mixture, beginning and ending with the dry ingredients. This will ensure that your cupcakes have a light and fluffy texture.

Once your batter is mixed, it is time to fill your cupcake liners. Using a spoon or an ice cream scoop, fill each liner about two-thirds full. This will allow room for the cupcakes to rise without overflowing.

Now it's time to bake your cupcakes. Place the filled cupcake pans in the preheated oven and set a timer for the recommended baking time. Cupcakes typically bake for around 15-20 minutes, but this can vary depending on your recipe and oven. To check if your cupcakes are done, insert a toothpick into the center of a cupcake. If it comes out clean or with a few crumbs, your cupcakes are ready. If the toothpick comes out with wet batter, continue baking for a few more minutes.

Once your cupcakes are baked, remove them from the oven and let them cool in the pans for a few minutes."

"Essential Ingredients and Equipment of Cupcake Baking: Cupcake baking is a delightful and popular activity that allows individuals to create delicious and visually appealing treats. To successfully bake cupcakes, it is essential to have the right ingredients and equipment. This article will provide a comprehensive guide on the essential ingredients and equipment needed for cupcake baking.

Ingredients:

1. Flour: All-purpose flour is commonly used in cupcake recipes. It provides structure and stability to the cupcakes. It is important to measure the flour accurately to ensure the right texture.

2. Sugar: Granulated sugar is the most commonly used sweetener in cupcake recipes. It adds sweetness and helps to create a tender texture. Brown sugar can also be used for a richer flavor.

3. Butter: Unsalted butter is typically used in cupcake recipes. It adds moisture and richness to the cupcakes. It is important to use softened butter to ensure easy mixing.

4. Eggs: Eggs act as a binding agent and provide structure to the cupcakes. They also add moisture and richness. It is important to use room temperature eggs for better incorporation into the batter.

5. Baking powder and baking soda: These leavening agents help the cupcakes rise and create a light and fluffy texture. Baking powder is used in recipes that do not contain acidic ingredients, while baking soda

is used in recipes that contain acidic ingredients like buttermilk or yogurt.

6. Milk: Milk adds moisture and richness to the cupcakes. It is important to use whole milk or buttermilk for a tender texture.

7. Vanilla extract: Vanilla extract enhances the flavor of the cupcakes. It adds a subtle and sweet aroma to the baked goods.

8. Salt: Salt enhances the flavor of the cupcakes and balances the sweetness. It is important to use a small amount of salt to avoid overpowering the other flavors.

Equipment:

1. Mixing bowls: Mixing bowls are essential for combining the ingredients. It is recommended to have a variety of sizes to accommodate different recipes.

2. Electric mixer: An electric mixer makes the mixing process easier and faster. It helps to cream the butter and sugar, and incorporate the other ingredients evenly.

3. Measuring cups and spoons: Accurate measurement of ingredients is crucial for successful cupcake baking. Measuring cups and spoons are used to measure dry and liquid ingredients.

4. Cupcake liners: Cupcake liners are used to line the cupcake pans. They prevent the cupcakes from sticking to the pan and make it easier

to   remove   them   after   baking.

"Fundamental Techniques in Cupcake Making:

Cupcake making is a delightful and creative activity that allows individuals to showcase their baking skills and create delicious treats. Whether you are a beginner or an experienced baker, understanding the fundamental techniques in cupcake making is essential to achieve the perfect texture, flavor, and presentation.

One of the first fundamental techniques in cupcake making is properly measuring the ingredients. Baking is a science, and accurate measurements are crucial for achieving consistent results. Use measuring cups and spoons to ensure that you are adding the right amount of flour, sugar, butter, and other ingredients. It is also important to sift dry ingredients like flour and cocoa powder to remove any lumps and ensure even distribution.

Another important technique is creaming the butter and sugar. Creaming involves beating the butter and sugar together until they become light and fluffy. This process incorporates air into the mixture, resulting in a tender and moist cupcake. Use an electric mixer or stand mixer for this step, and be sure to scrape down the sides of the bowl to ensure all the ingredients are well combined.

The next technique is adding the eggs one at a time. Adding the eggs individually allows them to fully incorporate into the batter, preventing any curdling or separation. Beat each egg into the mixture until fully combined before adding the next one. This step ensures a smooth and cohesive batter.

Once the wet ingredients are combined, it's time to alternate adding the dry ingredients and the liquid. This technique helps to prevent overmixing, which can lead to a dense and tough cupcake. Start by adding a portion of the dry ingredients to the wet mixture, followed by a portion of the liquid. Gently fold the ingredients together using a spatula until just combined. Repeat this process until all the dry ingredients and liquid are incorporated.

Properly filling the cupcake liners is another important technique. Fill each liner about two-thirds full to allow room for the cupcakes to rise during baking. Using an ice cream scoop or a piping bag can help ensure consistent portion sizes and a neat appearance.

Baking time and temperature are crucial factors in achieving perfectly baked cupcakes. Preheat the oven to the recommended temperature stated in the recipe and set a timer to ensure accurate baking time. Overbaking can result in dry cupcakes, while underbaking can lead to a gooey or sunken center. Use a toothpick or cake tester to check for doneness. Insert it into the center of a cupcake."

"Tips for Baking the Perfect Cupcake Every Time: Baking the perfect cupcake every time can be a delightful and rewarding experience. Whether you are a seasoned baker or just starting out, there are a few tips and tricks that can help you achieve cupcake perfection. From choosing the right ingredients to mastering the baking process, here are some key tips to ensure your cupcakes turn out moist, fluffy, and delicious every single time.

1. Start with quality ingredients: The first step to baking the perfect cupcake is to use high-quality ingredients. This includes fresh eggs, unsalted butter, and pure vanilla extract. Using fresh ingredients will not only enhance the flavor of your cupcakes but also contribute to their overall texture.

2. Measure accurately: Baking is a science, and accurate measurements are crucial for achieving consistent results. Invest in a good set of measuring cups and spoons, and make sure to level off your dry ingredients with a straight edge. This will ensure that your cupcakes rise evenly and have the right balance of flavors.

3. Don't overmix the batter: Overmixing the batter can lead to dense and tough cupcakes. Mix the ingredients just until they are combined, and avoid overworking the batter. This will help to create a light and tender texture in your cupcakes.

4. Use room temperature ingredients: It is important to use room temperature ingredients, especially butter and eggs, as they will blend together more easily and result in a smoother batter. Take your ingredients out of the refrigerator at least 30 minutes before you start baking.

5. Preheat your oven: Preheating your oven is essential for even baking. Make sure to preheat your oven to the specified temperature in the recipe before you start mixing your ingredients. This will ensure that your cupcakes bake evenly and rise properly.

6. Use the right baking tools: Investing in good quality baking tools can make a significant difference in the outcome of your cupcakes. Use a sturdy muffin tin with non-stick coating or line it with cupcake liners to prevent sticking. Additionally, use an ice cream scoop or a piping bag to evenly distribute the batter into the cupcake liners for consistent results.

7. Fill the cupcake liners correctly: Fill the cupcake liners about two-thirds full to allow room for the cupcakes to rise. Overfilling the liners can cause the batter to spill over and result in unevenly shaped cupcakes.

8. Rotate the pan halfway through baking: To ensure even baking, rotate the cupcake pan halfway through the baking time."

"Storing and Transporting Cupcakes: When it comes to storing and transporting cupcakes, there are a few key considerations to keep in mind to ensure that your sweet treats arrive at their destination in perfect condition. Cupcakes are delicate and can easily be damaged if not handled properly, so it's important to take the necessary precautions.

First and foremost, it's crucial to choose the right container for storing and transporting cupcakes. Opt for a sturdy and secure container that is specifically designed for cupcakes. These containers typically have individual compartments to hold each cupcake in place, preventing them from moving around and getting damaged during transit. Additionally, make sure the container has a tight-fitting lid to keep the cupcakes fresh and secure.

If you don't have a cupcake container, you can also use a regular airtight container or a cake carrier with adjustable inserts. Just make sure to place each cupcake in a separate compartment or use dividers to prevent them from touching each other. This will help maintain their shape and prevent any frosting or decorations from smudging.

Before placing the cupcakes in the container, it's important to let them cool completely. Warm cupcakes can create condensation, which can make the frosting melt and ruin the appearance of the cupcakes. Once cooled, carefully place each cupcake in its designated compartment, making sure they are not overcrowded.

To further protect the cupcakes during transportation, you can use additional cushioning. Place a layer of tissue paper or parchment paper between the cupcakes and the lid of the container to provide extra protection and prevent any movement. You can also place a non-slip mat or a damp towel at the bottom of the container to prevent the cupcakes from sliding around.

When it comes to transporting the cupcakes, it's essential to handle the container with care. Keep it level and avoid any sudden movements or tilting that could cause the cupcakes to shift or topple over. If you're transporting the cupcakes in a car, place the container on a flat surface, such as the floor of the passenger seat or in the trunk, to minimize any potential movement.

If you're transporting the cupcakes over a longer distance or in hot weather, it's advisable to keep them refrigerated. However, it's important to note that refrigeration can affect the texture and taste of the cupcakes, so it's best to refrigerate them only if absolutely necessary.

In conclusion, storing and transporting cupcakes requires careful attention to detail to ensure that they arrive at their destination in perfect condition."

"Crafting Luxurious Cupcake Creations: Crafting Luxurious Cupcake Creations is a delightful and creative process that involves the art of baking and decorating cupcakes to perfection. It requires a keen eye for detail, a passion for culinary excellence, and a touch of imagination to create cupcakes that not only taste heavenly but also look visually stunning.

To begin the process of crafting luxurious cupcake creations, one must first gather the necessary ingredients. This typically includes flour, sugar, butter, eggs, milk, and various flavorings such as vanilla or chocolate. The quality of these ingredients is crucial in achieving a delectable taste and texture in the cupcakes.

Once the ingredients are assembled, the baking process begins. This involves carefully measuring and mixing the ingredients to create a smooth and consistent batter. The batter is then poured into cupcake liners and placed in the oven to bake. The cupcakes must be monitored closely to ensure they are baked to perfection, with a golden brown color and a moist, fluffy interior.

While the cupcakes are baking, attention can be turned to the creative aspect of crafting luxurious cupcake creations - the decoration. This is where the true artistry comes into play. Various techniques can be employed to elevate the appearance of the cupcakes, such as piping intricate designs with buttercream frosting, using fondant to create decorative shapes and figures, or even adding edible glitter or pearls for a touch of glamour.

The choice of flavors and fillings also plays a significant role in creating luxurious cupcake creations. From classic flavors like vanilla or chocolate to more exotic options like salted caramel or raspberry, the possibilities are endless. Fillings such as fruit preserves, chocolate ganache, or cream cheese add an extra layer of indulgence and surprise when biting into the cupcake.

Furthermore, the presentation of these luxurious cupcake creations is equally important. They can be displayed on elegant tiered stands, adorned with delicate floral arrangements, or packaged in beautifully designed boxes, making them perfect for special occasions or as gifts.

Crafting luxurious cupcake creations is not just about the end result; it is a labor of love and a way to express creativity and passion for baking. It is an opportunity to bring joy and delight to those who indulge in these delectable treats. Whether it's a wedding, a birthday celebration, or simply a sweet treat for oneself, these luxurious cupcakes are sure to leave a lasting impression and create unforgettable memories."

Introduction

Cupcakes, they are cute, extremely easy to make and have taken the world by storm in the last few years. There is little doubt that this cute treat often reserved for children, has become a staple of many parties for both the young and the old.

And what is not to like about cupcakes. They are usually very easy to make – a touch of batter, a few tools and in less than 30 minutes, you can be eating a moist cake treat. In addition, you can really play around with the decorating. Really, there is nothing that you can dislike and you can make them as decadent or as simple as you like.

For me, cupcakes are the go to treat. I can make some spectacular cupcakes with nothing more than a few ingredients and they rarely take the same amount of time to decorate as a cake. Kids love them and most adults enjoy them too.

Whether you are new to baking or an experienced baker, this book is designed to bring you some of the best cupcake recipes that you can make. All are extremely tasty and they really take no time at all. The steps are simply and anyone can create an amazing treat even if they have never baked before.

Care has been taken to take cupcakes to a different level and along with basic recipes; you can find some truly amazing decadent recipes. In addition, vegan cupcakes and low fat cupcakes are included in this book for anyone looking for a treat while still watching the foods that they are eating.

In the end, what you will find in this book is a resource that will help you make, decorate and enjoy some cute little creations from your kitchen.

The Great Big World of Cupcakes

Although the title to this chapter is the great big world of cupcakes, I would like to remind you that cupcakes are pretty small and you don't need to do much too really enjoy them.

What everyone who starts baking cupcakes should realize is that anything baked in a cupcake tin can be a cupcake. You can make them with pie crust, as cheesecakes or as brownies but the main point to a cupcake is that it is a small dessert that everyone can enjoy.

In addition, these recipes don't have to be cupcake recipes and for anyone just starting out in the world of cupcakes, you can use traditional cake recipes or any type of baking recipe.

There isn't a lot of information that you need to start baking your own cupcakes but I do recommend that you read through all the tips in this book for some insight. When baking, make sure you place the baking tin in the center of the oven and that you turn them during baking for the best distribution of heat. In addition, always fill the tins to ¾ full and check your baking often.

If you do these things, your cupcakes will be perfect – especially when you follow the recipes in this book.

Tools for Making Cupcakes

Tools that you need for making cupcakes are actually quite simple and you really don't need to have a lot of things in your home. To put it simply, all you need is a cupcake tin and a few bowls and this is often the draw for cupcakes.

For those who are just starting out in the world of baking, here is a list of cake baking tools and cupcake tools that you should try to have on hand.

- **Measuring Cups:** Used for baking, I recommend that you have several cups where the measurements are at the top of the cup. So have a ¼ cup, ½ cup, etc. This will ensure that your measurements are perfect.

- **Measuring Spoons:** Again, choose measuring spoons that are individual measurements. It is often a good idea to have two different measuring spoon sets, one for dry and one for wet ingredients.

- **Mixing Bowls:** I always recommend that you have at least 3 mixing bowls of various sizes but it is better if you have more than that as you will usually use them when baking. I also recommend having a few glass or metal bowls available for when you make whipped cream or mix cold ingredients.

- **Electric Mixer:** Whether you have a stand mixer or an electric mixer, it is important to have some way to mix your various mixtures without using a hand whisk. If you have a mixer, the end result will be much nicer than if you hand mix your ingredients.

- **Food Processor:** You can also use a blender but you want to have something that will help puree fruit if you are using it for cupcake fillings...and yes, you can fill cupcakes.

- **Cupcake Liners:** Paper liners that you use to keep the cupcakes from sticking to the sides of the pan. They are optional but I find they make baking cupcakes much easier.

- **_Cupcake Tins:_** It is important to have a wide range of cupcake tins for making cupcake. Play around with size from mini to jumbo and also have shaped cupcake tins to add a different sense of style to your treats.

- **_Decorating Bags and Tips:_** These aren't always necessary but if you would like to decorate your cupcakes, I recommend having a set of decorating bags and tips.

- **_Injector Tip:_** While this can be placed in the same group as decorating tips, injector tips are used when you want to inject a filling into the center of a cupcake.

- **_Double Boiler:_** A double boiler is a pot that fits into a larger pot so you can place water in the bottom one and melt chocolate in the top pot. If you do not want to invest in a double boiler, you can use a large pot and place a can or a heat safe glass bowl into the bowling water to make your own double boiler. Be careful when you do this as some glass bowls can rupture if the heat is too high.

- **_Parchment Paper:_** For covering your pans during baking or when you need to chill the cake pops.

- **_Spatulas:_** Have a number of different spatulas for smoothing out your toppings.

- **_Zester:_** Finally, have a zester for your lemons and oranges.

And that is really all you need to make your own cupcakes. There are many different types of tools that you can purchase to make your kitchen state of the art, however, don't feel as though you need to make a huge investment when you first start making your own desserts.

Decorating Tips for Cupcakes

The final thing that I want to look at before you start baking your own cupcakes is a number of tips you can use for decorating. Although we often think of cakes as the baked good you decorate, cupcakes are very easy to decorate and you can really play around with the way you decorate.

For those of you interested in decorating your cupcakes, here are a few tips for you to follow.

Tip Number One: Understand how to apply Icing to Cupcakes

First, you should understand how to apply icing to cupcakes. Although you can just pipe the icing on, I find that the end result looks much better if you apply a very thin layer of icing with a knife. Once you have done that, you can start piping on the designs. Some designs are:

1M Swirl: This is a swirl that uses the 1M decorating tip. It looks like an ice cream when you are finished and is the most popular choice for piping since it is very easy to do and has a nice end result. To make this swirl, hold the tip at a 90° angle to the cupcake about a ¼ inch above it. Start at the outer edge and pipe in a swirl to the center, pulling up at the end for an elevated look. Stop applying pressure on the bag and then remove the tip from the cupcake.

Rosette: Very simple to do, the rosette should be started about an 8th of an inch above the cupcake. Squeeze the frosting and make a small circle, move back to the center and then stop squeezing the frosting.

Star: Another popular one, you can use a large number of stars to fill a cupcake and to create your own design. Start with the piping bag at a 90° angle and begin to squeeze when the tip is an 8th of an inch from the cupcake. Squeeze the frosting out until you have the size you want.

Tip Number Two: Think outside the Box

Don't feel like you need to stick with the ordinary when it comes to decorating your cupcakes. Some great ways to decorate are:

- **Cupcake Pictures:** You create a design and then place the cupcakes side by side. Decorate in different colors to recreate your design such as a large happy face. The majority of the cupcakes should be yellow with a few black so you have the eyes and mouth.

- **Use the Cupcake:** Don't worry about cutting into your cupcakes at all. You can create some interesting designs, such as a butterfly, by adding parts of the cupcake onto the top of the frosting.

- **Make them into something:** You can make just about anything from popular character items such as a Pokémon ball, or an angry bird, to cute little animals such as a puppy dog face. The sky really is the limit with decorating.

Tip Number Three: Decorate with more than just Icing

In many of the recipes in this book, I mention garnishes for your cupcakes and you should really think about using more than just icing for your cupcakes. This gives you an additional treat on your cupcake and it also allows you to add to your designs. Some items to decorate with are:

- *__Fruit:__* A raspberry in the center of the frosting for your raspberry cupcakes is perfect but you can use fruit for any type of cupcake. With fruit, make sure it is a variety that doesn't discolor easily and also one that compliments your cupcake flavor.

- *__Candy:__* I love putting candy on cupcakes and you can use them as either a garnish or as a tie in for your design. Long string licorice can be an antenna for your butterflies or a gum drop can be a nose. With candy, make sure you attach them to the cupcake with icing or they won't stick.

- *__Sprinkles:__* Sprinkles, silver balls, and all the other items that can be sprinkled onto the cake can be an excellent way to add a bit of whimsy to your cupcakes.

Tip Number Four: Decorate with Height

Since you are working with a very small canvas when you decorate a cupcake, make sure you play with the height. Don't keep the icing flush with the cupcake but instead, create some levels to it. You can also add some levels with candy and the other items you use to embellish your cupcakes.

Tip Number Five: Don't Forget Simplicity

The last tip that I recommend is that you remember how simple cupcakes are and not go too far with the decorating. A swirl of icing may be all you need to make your cupcake perfect so don't feel the need to overdress your cupcakes if the occasion doesn't call for it.

Now that we have delved into the world of cupcakes and have gone over what you will need to make them, it is time to look at the many different types of recipes that you can use.

Recipes

In this section of the book, I have gone over a number of different recipes that range from easy, no fuss recipes to more complex recipes. In addition, there are a few recipes that are vegan as well as low-fat so you can enjoy the decadence of cupcakes without gaining those few extra pounds.

Frosting Recipes

Before we get into the actual recipes for the cupcakes themselves, we need to have a few frosting and icing recipes. You don't have to ice or frost your cupcakes but they definitely make for a much tastier treat if you do. Although you can use store bought frosting and icing, homemade frosting is actually very easy and usually tastes a 100 times better.

Simply White Frosting

Basic white frosting is a very versatile frosting that you can use for decorating or even as an extra filling. If you use it for decorating, you can color it to match your design with very little difficulty. This frosting is light and creamy.

For a more uniformed color to your frosting, add the food coloring to the water before mixing it into the dry ingredients.

Ingredients:

Dry:

- 1 cup of white sugar
- ¼ tsp of cream of tartar

Wet:

- 1/3 cup of water
- 1 tsp of vanilla extract
- 2 egg whites

Directions:

1. In a large saucepan, whisk together the water and sugar.

2. Place on the stove and set the temperature to medium high.

3. Add in the cream of tartar.

4. Cook until the sugar is completely dissolved, remove from the heat and set aside.

5. In a large mixing bowl, whip the egg whites.

6. Add the vanilla to the egg whites and then whip the ingredients until soft peaks begin to form.

7. Slowly add the sugar to the egg whites and continue to mix on high for roughly 10 minutes or until the frosting forms stiff peaks.

8. Use to frost your refrigerator cakes.

Decadent Butter Cream Icing

Butter cream icing is a favorite for many people because of its rich, buttery flavor. It usually has a nice texture and thickness to it and can be a very nice icing for decorating.

Baking Tips, Tricks and Hints

When creaming butter, shortening or cream cheese, cut the ingredients with a pastry cutter or two knives before creaming. This makes it much easier and will help avoid lumps in your ingredients.

Ingredients:

Dry:

- 4 cups of icing sugar

Wet:

- 2 tbsp of milk
- ½ cup of butter
- ½ cup of shortening
- 1 tsp of vanilla extract

Directions:

1. In a large mixing bowl, cream together the shortening and butter.

2. Fold in the vanilla and mix until the ingredients are smooth.

3. Add one cup of icing sugar to the mixture and blend completely.

4. Repeat, adding one cup at a time. Make sure the icing sugar is fully incorporated before adding the next cup.

5. Add the milk and continue blending until the icing is light and fluffy.

Chocoholic Icing

For any chocolate lover out there, a tasty chocolate icing is a must have in their array of recipes and this frosting recipe is sure to delight even the pickiest of chocolate lovers. The rich blend offers just enough chocolate without going overboard and goes perfectly with a large number of cupcakes.

Baking Tips, Tricks and Hints

When icing, apply a thin layer of icing to the cake before adding the thicker layer, this will give you a better looking cupcake.

Ingredients:

Dry:

- 2 ¾ cups of icing sugar
- 6 tbsp of cocoa powder, unsweetened

Wet:

- 5 tbsp of evaporated milk
- 6 tbsp of butter
- 1 tsp of vanilla extract

Directions:

1. In a large bowl, cream the butter until it is smooth.

2. In a separate bowl, sift together the icing sugar and cocoa powder.

3. Add a cup of the sugar mixture to the butter.

4. Pour in two tablespoons of evaporated milk.

5. Mix until the ingredients are fully incorporated.

6. Repeat until all of the milk and icing sugar has been added to the butter.

7. Fold in the vanilla.

8. Continue mixing until you have an icing that is light and fluffy.

Decorator's Choice Royal Icing

Royal icing is not usually a frosting that you use for covering the cake since it hardens. Instead, use it to make decorations for your cupcakes.

Baking Tips, Tricks and Hints

If you find your frosting is too dry, add more milk or water to it. Generally, playing with a recipe will give you the desired results.

Ingredients:

Dry:

- 4 cups of icing sugar
- 3 tbsp of meringue powder

Wet:

- 6 tbsp of water

Directions:

1. In a large bowl, sift the icing sugar.

2. Whisk in the meringue powder.

3. Add the water and mix at a low speed until peaks begin to form. This usually takes about 7 to 10 minutes.

4. Decorate. Since this icing does dry very quickly, keep a wet kitchen towel over the bowl at all times to keep it moist.

Move over Cheesecake Cream Cheese Frosting

One of the more popular choices for frosting, cream cheese frosting is very rich and has a creamy, thick texture to it. Like basic white frosting, cream cheese frosting is very easy to color so your refrigerator cakes can match any event that you are making them for.

Baking Tips, Tricks and Hints

When you are frosting with a spatula, make sure you wipe the spatula each time you remove it from the cake. This will prevent crumbs from getting onto the icing.

Ingredients:

Dry:

- 2 cups of icing sugar

Wet:

- 16 oz of cream cheese
- ½ cup of butter
- 1 tsp of vanilla extract

Directions:

1. In a large mixing bowl, cream together the cheese and butter. Mix until it is creamy and smooth.

2. Fold in the vanilla and mix until it is well blended.

3. Sift the icing sugar into a separate bowl.

4. Gradually add it to the cream cheese mixture.

5. Blend until the frosting is smooth and creamy.

Finishing Touches Fondant

If you love making little embellishments for your cupcakes, then this is a recipe that you should have. This fondant is very easy to make and it creates a beautifully finished cupcake.

Baking Tips, Tricks and Hints

Make smaller batches of fondant and add food coloring to have a wide range of colors to work with.

Ingredients:

Dry:

- 3 cups of icing sugar
- ½ tsp of salt

Wet:

- 1 cup of shortening
- 1 cup of light corn syrup
- 1 tsp of clear vanilla extract

Directions:

1. In a large mixing bowl, cream together the shortening and corn syrup until it is smooth.

2. Add the salt and mix until it is incorporated.

3. Fold in the vanilla, again, mixing until it is blended. If you are adding color, add it at this point.

4. Sift the icing sugar into a separate bowl.

5. Slowly add the icing sugar to the shortening mixture.

6. Once it gets too hard to mix, turn it out onto a clean, flat surface that has been dusted with icing sugar and knead.

7. Add more icing sugar as needed until you have smooth dough that is not sticky.

8. Roll out until it is 1/8th of an inch in thickness.

9. Drape over the cake pop and smooth the seams.

10. Store in airtight containers in either the fridge or at room temperature.

The Basic Recipes

Basic is Best White Cupcakes

Basic white cupcakes are almost a staple in the cupcake world and really, there is no way that you can go wrong with these cupcakes. They have a simple taste that is the perfect flavor on its own or as a starting point for a variety of other flavors.

Baking Tips, Tricks and Hints

Keep your cupcakes moist by leaving two tins empty in your cupcake pan. Fill the empty tins with water and the rest of the cupcakes will be sublime.

Ingredients:
Dry:
- 1 ½ cups of flour
- 1 cup of white sugar
- 1 ¾ tsp of baking powder

Wet:
- ½ cup of milk
- 2 tsp of vanilla

- ½ cup of butter
- 2 eggs

Directions:

1. In a large mixing bowl, sift together the flour and baking powder.

2. Whisk in the white sugar. Set aside.

3. In a separate bowl, cream the butter.

4. Add in the first egg and mix until it is fully incorporated.

5. Add the second egg to the butter mixture and again, mix until it is fully incorporated.

6. Fold in the vanilla and milk and continue mixing until the butter mixture is well blended.

7. Slowly add the wet ingredients to the dry.

8. Mix until the ingredients are smooth.

9. Pour into a prepared cupcake tin that has been lightly floured and greased or lined with cupcake liners.

10. Bake at 350°F for 15 to 20 minutes or until the middle of the cake springs back when touched.

Chocolate Lover's Cupcakes

Chocolate is a must have for many people but there is no reason to go overboard with the rich flavoring. The chocolate levels in this cake are sure to please everyone, whether they are a chocoholic or someone who only likes chocolate a little.

Baking Tips, Tricks and Hints

Always use ingredients that are room temperature unless a recipe calls for something different. This will give you the best consistency and will help with mixing the ingredients together.

Ingredients:

Dry:

- 2 cups of flour
- 1 tsp of baking soda
- ½ tsp of baking powder
- 2 cups of white sugar
- ¾ tsp of salt
- 5 oz of dark chocolate

Wet:

- 1 cup of water
- ½ cup of milk
- 1 tsp of vanilla
- ½ cup of butter
- 2 eggs

Directions:

1. In a double boiler, carefully melt the chocolate. Set aside.

2. Sift together the flour, baking soda, baking powder and salt.

3. Whisk the sugar into the flour mixture.

4. In a separate bowl, mix together the water, milk and vanilla.

5. Add in the 2 eggs and combine until they are well blended.

6. Add the butter to the egg mixture and mix until the ingredients are thoroughly mixed.

7. Fold in the melted dark chocolate.

8. Pour the egg mixture into the flour mixture.

9. Mix until the batter is smooth but make sure you do not over mix.

10. Pour into a prepared cupcake tin that has been lightly floured and greased or lined with cupcake liners.

11. Bake at 350°F for 25 to 30 minutes or until the middle of the cupcake springs back when touched.

Vanilla Dream Cupcakes

Although a lot of the recipes in this book use vanilla, there is an extra zip to the flavor in these cupcakes. Definitely a treat everyone will love, this recipe is another basic recipe that can be dressed up or simply left on its own.

Baking Tips, Tricks and Hints

Use pure vanilla instead of artificial for better flavor in your cupcakes.

Ingredients:

Dry:

- 2 cups of flour
- 3 tsp of baking powder
- 1 ½ cups of white sugar
- ½ tsp of salt

Wet:

- 1 cup of milk
- ½ cup of vegetable shortening
- 3 tsp of pure vanilla
- 2 eggs
- 4 egg whites

Directions:

1. Sift together the flour, baking powder and salt.

2. Whisk the sugar into the flour mixture.

3. In a separate bowl, cream together the vanilla and shortening.

4. Fold in the milk and continue to mix until they are thoroughly mixed

5. Add in the 2 eggs and combine until they are well blended.

6. Separate the remaining eggs so that you have a bowl of egg whites. You will need 4 large egg whites. Throw away the egg yolks.

7. Pour the egg whites into the batter and blend for about 2 minutes on a low speed.

8. Fold in the flour ingredients slowly, mixing as you do.

9. Mix until the batter is smooth.

10. Pour into a prepared cupcake tin that has been lightly floured and greased or lined with cupcake liners.

11. Bake at 350°F for 20 to 25 minutes or until a toothpick inserted in the middle of the cupcake comes out clean.

12. Cool for 10 minutes in the pan and then cool completely on a wire rack.

Devilishly Good Cupcakes

Create some devilishly tasty cupcakes with this wonderful recipe that is full of flavor and excitement. Like most of the basic cupcake recipe, this cake is perfect on its own but can really be dressed up to compliment anything.

Baking Tips, Tricks and Hints

Be sure to preheat the oven before baking a cake. This will give you the proper consistency and will prevent the cake from not cooking properly or burning.

Ingredients:
Dry:

- 2 ¼ cups of flour
- 1 ½ tsp of baking soda
- 2 cups of white sugar
- ¼ tsp of salt
- 3 oz of unsweetened chocolate

Wet:

- 1 cup of warm water
- ¼ cup of milk

- ½ cup of butter
- 1 tsp of white vinegar
- 2 eggs

Directions:

1. In a double boiler, melt the butter.

2. Add in the unsweetened chocolate and cook until it is melted and blended with the butter. Set aside.

3. In a large mixing bowl, cream together the sugar and eggs.

4. Fold in the slightly cooled chocolate mixture to the eggs and mix until it is just blended.

5. Add the warm water and mix until it is smooth.

6. In a separate bowl, sift together the flour, salt and baking soda.

7. Add a quarter of the flour mixture to the chocolate mixture, blend until the ingredients are incorporated. Repeat, adding a quarter of flour each time and making sure all the ingredients are wet.

8. In a separate bowl, whisk together the milk and vinegar. Add it to the chocolate batter and blend completely until the batter is smooth.

9. Pour into a prepared cupcake tin that has been lightly floured and greased or lined with cupcake liners.

10. Bake at 350°F for 25 to 30 minutes or until a toothpick inserted in the middle of the cake comes out clean.

11. Remove and allow to cool in the tins for 10 minutes before placing them on a wire rack to cool completely.

Light and Fluffy Yellow Cupcakes

If you were to ask me what my favorite type of cupcake is, I would have to say this light and fluffy yellow cupcake. It has enough taste to stand on its own and you can really play with the frostings to have a myriad of tastes in whatever you design. In addition, there is something so cheerful about any type of cupcake you make with it.

Baking Tips, Tricks and Hints

For better texture, always sift your flour twice.

Ingredients:

Dry:

- 2 cups of flour
- 2 tsp of baking powder
- 1 cup of white sugar
- ½ tsp of salt

Wet:

- ¾ cup of milk
- 2 tsp of vanilla
- ½ cup of butter
- 3 eggs

Directions:

1. In a large mixing bowl, sift together the flour, baking powder and salt. Set aside

2. In a separate bowl, cream together the sugar and butter. Blend until the mixture is fluffy.

3. Add an egg to the butter mixture.

4. Beat the egg until it is fully incorporated.

5. Repeat with the second egg and then the third making sure each egg is fully incorporated before adding the next egg.

6. Add a 1/3 of the flour to the butter mixture, mix until the ingredients are wet.

7. Add in a ¼ cup of milk, again mixing thoroughly.

8. Repeat this process with a 1/3 of the flour and a ¼ cup of the milk until the ingredients are fully added and the batter is smooth.

9. Pour into a prepared cupcake tin that has been lightly floured and greased or lined with cupcake liners.

10. Bake at 350°F for 20 to 25 minutes or until a toothpick inserted in the middle of the cake comes out clean.

11. Remove and allow to cool in the tins for 10 minutes before placing them on a wire rack to cool completely.

Silky Dream Red Velvet Cupcakes

Any time there is a holiday; I usually pull out this recipe, grab a white cream cheese frosting and bake some sweet little red velvet cupcakes. The vibrant red makes it an ideal cupcake for Christmas or Valentine's Day treats and the white cream cheese creates a startling contrast. Even with different frostings, people usually love this brightly colored treat.

Baking Tips, Tricks and Hints

When you are baking cupcakes, only fill the cupcake tin to 2/3rds full. This will give you a nice finished product with a very good cupcake top.

Ingredients:

Dry:

- 2 cups of flour
- 1 ½ tsp of baking soda
- 1 ½ cups of white sugar
- 1 tsp of salt
- 1/3 cup of cocoa powder, unsweetened

Wet:

- 1 cup of buttermilk
- 1 tsp of vanilla

- ½ cup of butter
- 1 tbsp of white vinegar
- 1 ounce of red food coloring
- 2 eggs

Directions:

1. In a large mixing bowl, sift together your flour and salt.

2. Whisk in the cocoa powder and set aside.

3. In another large mixing bowl, cream together the sugar and butter until it is fluffy.

4. Add the eggs and mix until they are well blended.

5. In a separate bowl, combine the vanilla, buttermilk and food coloring. Blend until you have a bright red buttermilk mixture.

6. Pour into the butter mixture and mix until the ingredients are smooth.

7. In another bowl, mix together the vinegar and baking soda and pour it into the butter mixture before the fizzing has stopped.

8. Fold the flour mixture into the batter and mix until it is blended.

9. Pour into a prepared cupcake tin that has been lightly floured and greased or lined with cupcake liners.

10. Bake at 350°F for 20 to 25 minutes or until a toothpick inserted in the middle of the cake comes out clean.

11. Remove and allow to cool in the tins for 10 minutes before placing them on a wire rack to cool completely.

Sweet and Spongy Cupcakes

Sweet, spongy and the perfect cake base for any type of cupcake, this is very similar to yellow cake, however, the texture is slightly different. One of the best parts of this cake is that it is not overly sweet so you can really enjoy a few cupcakes without feeling too guilty.

Baking Tips, Tricks and Hints

Always cool your cupcakes in the pan for 5 to 10 minutes before turning them out onto a wire rack. This will give you the best finished product.

Ingredients:

Dry:

- 2 cups of flour
- 2 tsp of baking powder
- 1 cup of white sugar
- ¼ tsp of salt

Wet:

- ½ tsp of vanilla
- 1 cup of butter
- 2 tsp of lemon juice
- 2 tbsp of warm water

- 4 eggs
- Lemon Zest (usually ½ a lemon)

Directions:

1. Zest the lemon and place it into a blender.

2. Pour in the sugar and blend until the ingredients are full blended.

3. Pour the lemon zest mixture into a large bowl.

4. Add the butter and cream the butter and sugar together until it is fluffy.

5. Slowly add the eggs to the mixture. Start with one egg and mix it in completely. Add the second egg and repeat. Do not mix in all the eggs at once.

6. Pour in the water, lemon juice and vanilla and blend completely.

7. In a separate bowl, sift the flour, baking powder and salt together.

8. Add half of the flour mixture to the sugar mixture and mix until the ingredients are fully incorporated.

9. Add the rest of the flour to the mixture and blend until the cake batter becomes shiny. This usually takes about 10 to 15 minutes of mixing on medium speed.

10. Pour into a prepared cupcake tin that has been lightly floured and greased or lined with cupcake liners.

11. Bake at 350°F for 20 to 25 minutes or until a toothpick inserted in the middle of the cake comes out clean.

12. Remove and allow to cool in the tins for 10 minutes before placing them on a wire rack to cool completely.

Citrus Breeze Orange Cupcakes

Although orange isn't usually what you think of when you think of a basic cupcake, this fruity cupcake is an excellent choice since it is easy to make. It can be a perfect cupcake on its own without any icing or you can dress them up for a sweet dessert.

Baking Tips, Tricks and Hints

Use cupcake liners in your tins to prevent the cupcakes from sticking to the side of the pans.

Ingredients:

Dry:

- 1 ¾ cups of flour
- 2 ½ tsp of baking powder
- 1 cup of white sugar
- ½ tsp of salt

Wet:

- ¼ cup of butter
- ½ cup of orange juice
- 1 tsp of vanilla extract
- 2 eggs

Directions:

1. In a large mixing bowl, cream together the butter and sugar.

2. Slowly add in the vanilla and continue to blend.

3. Separate your egg whites and egg yolks. Set the egg whites to the side.

4. Add the egg yolks to your sugar mixture and blend thoroughly.

5. In a separate bowl, sift together the flour, salt and baking powder.

6. Add a third of the dry ingredients to the butter mixture and stir.

7. Fold in 1/3 of the orange juice and mix completely.

8. Repeat, alternating between the dry ingredients and the orange juice until the ingredients are fully incorporated.

9. Mix the egg white until they are frothy.

10. Fold them into the cake batter. Mix until the batter is smooth.

11. Pour into a prepared cupcake tin that has been lightly floured and greased or lined with cupcake liners.

12. Bake at 350°F for 10 to 15 minutes or until a toothpick inserted in the middle of the cake comes out clean.

13. Remove and allow to cool in the tins for 10 minutes before placing them on a wire rack to cool completely.

Less than a Pound Cupcakes

A very rich and filling pound cake, this type of cake was originally named pound cake because of the amount of ingredients used, which was a pound. Today, the cakes are made in much smaller portions and you can now make them in cupcakes but the result is still a very delicious cake that has a wonderful texture to it.

Baking Tips, Tricks and Hints

Measuring is better done when you spoon the ingredients into the measuring cup instead of scooping your cup into your ingredients.

Ingredients:

Dry:

- 1 ½ cups of flour
- 1 tsp of baking powder
- ¾ cups of white sugar
- ¼ tsp of salt

Wet:

- 3 tbsp of milk
- 1 ½ tsp of vanilla
- 13 tbsp of butter
- 3 eggs

Directions:

1. In a large bowl, sift together your flour, baking powder and salt.

2. Whisk in the sugar until the dry ingredients are completely blended.

3. In a separate bowl, whisk the eggs together.

4. Pour in the milk and vanilla extract and blend until the ingredients are fully incorporated. Set aside

5. Slowly add half of egg mixture to the dry ingredients, mixing as you do until the ingredients are moist.

6. Fold in half of the butter and continue to blend, again, until the butter is worked throughout the ingredients.

7.   Add the remaining egg mixture and butter to the ingredients, again, mixing until everything is well blended.

8.   Pour into a prepared cupcake tin that has been lightly floured and greased or lined with cupcake liners.

9.   Bake at 350°F for 20 to 25 minutes or until a toothpick inserted in the middle of the cake comes out clean.

10.   Remove and allow to cool in the tins for 10 minutes before placing them on a wire rack to cool completely.

Touched By an Angel Cupcakes

The final recipe in our basic cupcake recipes is definitely no slouch. This is a sweet and airy little cake that is perfect for any occasion. The cake itself is a wonderful treat and the taste is heavenly.

Baking Tips, Tricks and Hints

Tamp the cupcake tins down on a counter to even the cake batter in the pan. This will give you fewer air bubbles and will make a more uniformed cake.

Ingredients:

Dry:

- 1 ¼ cups of flour
- 1 ½ cups of white sugar
- ¼ tsp of salt
- 1 ½ tsp of cream of tartar

Wet:

- 1 ½ tsp of vanilla

- 12 eggs

Directions:

1. Separate your egg yolks from your egg whites. Throw away the egg yolks and set the egg whites to the side. It is better to use large eggs for this as you will need about 1 and a half cups of egg whites.

2. Pour the egg whites into a large mixing bowl; beat until the egg whites are frothy.

3. Add in the salt and cream of tartar, blend.

4. Fold in the vanilla.

5. Mix the egg white mixture until stiff peaks begin to form. This usually takes about 4 to 5 minutes of mixing.

6. Pour in a cup of the sugar and mix until the sugar is fully incorporated.

7. In a separate bowl, whisk together the sugar and flour.

8. Pour ¼ of the dry ingredients into the egg white mixture. Blend thoroughly.

9. Repeat, adding only a ¼ of the dry ingredients and mixing completely before adding the next amount of dry ingredients.

10. Pour into a prepared cupcake tin that has been lightly floured and greased or lined with cupcake liners.

11. Bake at 350°F for 20 to 25 minutes or until the tops of the cupcakes are golden brown and dry.

12. Remove and allow to cool in the tins for 10 minutes before placing them on a wire rack to cool completely.

The Decadent Recipes

While any type of cupcake recipe can be considered decadent, there are a few recipes that take cupcakes to a whole new level and makes them something even better. This section of the book will look at the truly decadent recipes that you can make.

Peanut Butter and Chocolate Cupcake

This is quite a recipe and not one I recommend for the new baker since there are a lot of extra steps. However, if you are up to the challenge, this is a treat everyone will be more than happy to eat.

Baking Tips, Tricks and Hints

Regardless of a recipe, you can play with different decorating ideas to put your own unique stamp on a recipe.

Ingredients:

Cupcakes:

Dry:

- ¾ cup of flour
- ¾ cup of white sugar
- ¾ tsp of baking powder
- ½ tsp of baking soda
- ½ tsp of salt
- 2 oz of bittersweet chocolate
- ½ cup of cocoa powder, unsweetened
- 15 mini Reese chocolate peanut butter cups

Wet:

- ½ cup of sour cream
- 8 tbsp of butter, unsalted
- 2 eggs

Frosting:

Dry:

- 2 cups of icing sugar

Wet:

- 2/3 cup of whipping cream
- 5 tbsp of butter, unsalted
- 1 cup of peanut butter, creamy

Glaze:

Dry:

- 5 oz of milk chocolate

Wet:

- ½ cup of coconut oil

Directions:

Cupcakes:

1. In a double boiler, add the butter and cocoa. Mix until well blended.

2. Chop the chocolate and place in the double boiler.

3. Cook on a medium low temperature, stirring constantly, until the chocolate is melted.

4. Remove from heat and cool until it is room temperature.

5. In a separate bowl, sift together the flour, baking powder and baking soda. Set aside.

6. In a large mixing bowl, whisk the eggs.

7. Add in the sugar and salt and blend until the ingredients are smooth.

8. Fold in the chocolate mixture and mix completely.

9.   Add 1/3 of the flour mixture, mixing until the ingredients are smooth.

10.   Fold in half of the sour cream, again, mixing completely.

11.   Repeat until all of the flour and sour cream is incorporated. The batter should be very thick, almost like a cookie batter.

12.   Spoon the batter into t a prepared cupcake tin that has been lightly floured and greased or lined with cupcake liners.

13.   Press a Reese peanut butter cup into the center of each cupcake tin. You want it to be level with the top of the cupcake batter.

14.   Bake at 350°F for 15 to 20 minutes or until a toothpick inserted into the top of the cake part (not the Reese cup) comes out clean.

15. Remove and allow to cool in the tins for 10 minutes before placing them on a wire rack to cool completely before frosting.

Frosting:

1. In a large mixing bowl, cream together the butter and peanut butter.

2. Add the icing sugar and blend until smooth.

3. Slowly pour in the cream and continue mixing until the mixture becomes light and creamy.

4. Allow to chill for about a half hour.

5. Pipe onto the cooled cupcakes.

Glaze:

1. In a double boiler, heat the coconut oil over medium low heat.

2. Chop up the chocolate.

3. Add chocolate to the double boiler and heat until the chocolate has melted.

4. Stir regularly to avoid over cooking the chocolate.

5. Remove from heat and allow to cool slightly.

6. Dip the top of the cupcakes, the frosting part, into the chocolate glaze.

7. Place in the fridge and allow it to chill for 20 minutes to set.

8. Serve.

Rose Flowered Cupcakes

There is always something wonderful about rose flavored treats and this treat is sure to bring anyone to a summer garden. The fresh taste and mouthwatering frosting is a perfect blend of sweetness and decadence.

Baking Tips, Tricks and Hints

Use a small amount of vegetable oil to add moisture to melted chocolate or candy melts if they are too hard.

Ingredients:

Cupcakes:

Dry:

- 2/3 cup of flour
- 1 ½ tsp of baking powder
- 2/3 cup of white sugar
- ¼ tsp of salt

- 5 tsp of dried rose petals, crushed

Wet:

- ¼ cup of margarine
- ½ cup of milk
- 1 tsp of rose water
- 3 eggs
- Pink food coloring

Frosting:

Dry:

- 4 cups of icing sugar
- Candied Rose Petals

Wet:

- ½ cup of butter
- ½ cup of shortening
- 1 tsp of rose water
- 5 tsp of milk
- Pink food coloring

Directions:

Cupcakes:

1. In a mixing bowl, sift together the salt, baking powder and flour.

2. Make a well in the dry ingredients and set aside.

3. In a separate bowl, whisk together the eggs and sugar.

4. Mix until it is light and fluffy.

5. Fold in the rose water and rose petals and mix completely.

6. Add food coloring until you get a rose pink color.

7. In a saucepan, set on the stove at medium low heat, boil the milk.

8. Add in the butter and stir until the butter is melted.

9. Pour the milk into the dry ingredients. Blend until the dry ingredients are moist.

10. Pour in the egg mixture, mix until the batter is smooth.

11. Pour into a prepared cupcake tin that has been lightly floured and greased or lined with cupcake liners.

12. Bake at 350°F for 10 to 15 minutes or until a toothpick inserted in the middle of the cake comes out clean.

13. Remove and allow to cool in the tins for 10 minutes before placing them on a wire rack to cool completely.

Frosting:

1. In a large mixing bowl, cream together the shortening and butter.

2. Mix until it is light and fluffy.

3. Add a cup of icing sugar and mix until it is completely incorporated.

4. Continue adding icing sugar, a cup at a time, until all of the icing sugar has been mixed thoroughly through the butter mixture.

5. Fold in the rose water and blend.

6. Slowly add the milk until the icing is smooth.

7. Add enough pink food coloring until you get a rose color.

8. Blend until the icing is light and fluffy.

9. Pipe onto the cupcakes and garnish with candied rose petals.

Shades of Black and White Cupcakes

Marbled cakes are always a hit with children and adults alike and this little cupcake, while not marbled, is a huge hit with everyone as well. Chocolate and vanilla abound and create a unique flavor that will have everyone asking for seconds.

Baking Tips, Tricks and Hints

Use glass or steel mixing bowls when you are mixing cold ingredients, especially for toppings. They hold the cold much longer and help create a perfect texture in your toppings.

Ingredients:

Cupcakes:

Dry:

- 1 cup of flour
- 1 cup of white sugar
- 2 ½ tsp of cocoa powder, unsweetened

Wet:

- 1 cup of margarine
- 1 tsp of vanilla
- 1 tbsp of milk
- 2 eggs

Frosting:

Dry:

- 1 1/3 cups of icing sugar

Wet:

- ¾ cup of margarine
- 1 ½ tsp of vanilla
- 2 ½ tbsp of milk
- 2 tbsp of cocoa powder, unsweetened

Directions:

Cupcakes:

1. In a mixing bowl, sift the flour.

2. Whisk in the cocoa powder. Set aside.

3. In a large mixing bowl, cream together the margarine and sugar. Mix until it is light and fluffy.

4. Add one egg and blend completely until it is fully incorporated.

5. Add the second egg, again, mixing completely.

6. Fold in the flour mixture and blend until the flour is moist.

7. Stir in the vanilla, mixing thoroughly.

8. Slowly add the milk until you have a soft, stiff batter. You may not need to use all of the milk to make this batter.

9. Pour into a prepared cupcake tin that has been lightly floured and greased or lined with cupcake liners.

10. Bake at 350˚F for 10 to 15 minutes or until a toothpick inserted in the middle of the cake comes out clean.

11. Remove and allow to cool in the tins for 10 minutes before placing them on a wire rack to cool completely.

Frosting:

1. In a large mixing bowl, cream together the margarine and icing sugar until it is smooth.

2. Add the milk and continue to mix until the mixture is light and fluffy.

3. Place the cocoa powder in a small bowl and add the boiling water.

4. Stir until you have a chocolate paste.

5. Fold the paste into the icing and add the vanilla.

6. Blend until the ingredients are smooth.

7. Pipe onto the cooled cupcakes and decorate with drizzled, melted chocolate.

Honey and Lavender Cupcakes

Floral cupcakes are truly divine but this lavender recipe takes that taste to a whole new level with the sweetness of honey. Perfect for any garden party or simply as an everyday treat.

Baking Tips, Tricks and Hints

To sweeten any type of fruit that you use, toss it in a few tablespoons of brown sugar. This will also help keep the fruit sweet tasting since baking will remove some of the sweetness.

Ingredients:

Cupcakes:

Dry:

- 1 1/3 cups of flour
- ½ cup of white sugar
- 1 ½ tsp of baking powder
- ¼ tsp of salt
- 5 tsp of honey
- 5 tsp of dried lavender flowers, crushed

Wet:

- ¼ cup of butter
- 1 tsp of vanilla
- ½ cup of milk
- 3 eggs

Frosting:

Dry:

- 1 cup of icing sugar

Wet:

- 1/3 cup of margarine
- 2 tbsp of milk
- 3 tsp of honey

Directions:

Cupcakes:

1. In a large mixing bowl, sift together the flour, salt and baking powder.

2. Make a well in the dry ingredients and set aside.

3. In a separate bowl, whisk together the eggs and sugar.

4. Mix until it is light and fluffy.

5. Fold in the honey and lavender petals and mix completely.

6. In a saucepan, set on the stove at medium low heat, boil the milk.

7. Add in the butter and stir until the butter is melted.

8. Pour the milk into the dry ingredients. Blend until the dry ingredients are moist.

9. Pour in the egg mixture, mix until the batter is smooth.

10. Pour into a prepared cupcake tin that has been lightly floured and greased or lined with cupcake liners.

11. Bake at 350°F for 10 to 15 minutes or until a toothpick inserted in the middle of the cake comes out clean.

12. Remove and allow to cool in the tins for 10 minutes before placing them on a wire rack to cool completely.

Frosting:

1. In a large mixing bowl, cream together the icing sugar and butter.

2. Mix until it is light and fluffy.

3. Fold in the honey and blend.

4. Slowly add the milk.

5. Blend until the icing is light and fluffy.

6. Pipe onto the cupcakes and garnish with candied lavender flowers petals.

Chocolate Chip Surprise

There is so much chocolaty goodness in this treat that one is usually enough for anyone. Whether you want it for a treat or as a decadent and playful dessert after a meal, this is the cupcake to suit all your tastes.

Baking Tips, Tricks and Hints

To make candied ingredients, slice the fruit or break the petals off of the flower so you have a very thin piece. Blanch in boiling water for 5 minutes. Drain the water and then return to heat with 1 cup of water and 1 ½ cups of sugar. Bring to a boil and then simmer for an hour. Remove from the juice and cool completely before using.

Ingredients:

Cupcakes:

Dry:

- 1 cup of flour
- 2 tbsp of flour
- 1/3 cup of white sugar
- 1 tbsp of white sugar
- 1/3 cup of brown sugar, packed
- 1 tbsp of brown sugar, packed
- ½ tsp of baking soda
- ½ tsp of salt

Wet:

- ½ cup of butter
- ½ tsp of vanilla
- 1 egg

Filling:

Dry:

- ½ cup of brown sugar, packed
- 1 cup of chocolate chips

- ½ cup of chopped nuts, unsalted
- Pinch of salt

Wet:

- 1 egg
- ½ tsp of vanilla

Directions:

Cupcakes:

1.   In a large mixing bowl, cream together the butter and brown and white sugars.

2.   Mix until it is light and fluffy.

3.   Add the vanilla and mix until fully incorporated.

4.   Add the egg and blend until smooth.

5.   In a separate bowl, sift together the salt, baking soda and flour.

6.   Slowly add the flour into the butter mixture.

7.   Blend until smooth.

8.   Pour into a prepared cupcake tin that has been lightly floured and greased or lined with cupcake liners.

9.   Bake at 350°F for 10.

10.   Remove from heat and top each cupcake with the filling.

11.   Return to the oven and bake for an additional 10 to 15 minutes or until a toothpick inserted into the center of the cupcake comes out clean.

12. Remove and allow to cool in the tins for 10 minutes before placing them on a wire rack to cool completely.

Filling:

1.   In a large mixing bowl, blend together the egg, salt and brown sugar.

2.   Fold in the vanilla and mix until the ingredients are smooth.

3.   Add the chocolate chips and stir until they dispersed through the filling.

4.   Fold in the nuts and mix until everything is well blended.

5.   Use in the cupcakes as directed.

Two Tone Cupcakes

While they may not be as decadent as some of the other recipes, this is a sweet little cupcake that can be mixed and matched to any type of occasion and you can really play with the colors.

Baking Tips, Tricks and Hints

Play with the colors of your batters to tie your cupcakes into a theme. Remember that cupcakes are all about fun.

Ingredients:

Dry:

- •   1 ¾ cups of cake flour
- •   1 cup of white sugar
- •   2 tsp of baking powder
- •   ½ tsp of salt
- •   1/3 cup of cocoa powder, unsweetened

Wet:

- •   1/3 cup of milk
- •   ¼ cup of boiling water

- ½ cup of butter, unsalted
- 1/3 cup of heavy cream
- 1 tsp of vanilla
- 3 eggs

Directions:

1. In a large mixing bowl, sift together the flour, salt and baking powder. Set aside.

2. In a separate bowl, whisk together the cream and milk. Set aside.

3. In a third bowl, cream together the butter and sugar.

4. Mix until it is light and fluffy.

5. Add an egg and mix until it is completely incorporated.

6. Add the second egg, again, mixing until it is well blended.

7. Add the final egg and mix until it is blended.

8. Fold in the vanilla and mix until the mixture is smooth.

9. Add in a third of the flour mixture and blend until the flour is moist.

10. Pour in half of the milk mixture. Blend completely.

11. Repeat the process, alternating the flour and milk, mixing completely between each addition.

12. Once you have a smooth batter, remove 1 cup of the batter.

13. In a separate bowl, mix together the cocoa powder and the boiling water.

14. Mix until you have a chocolate paste.

15. Fold the paste into the 1 cup of batter and mix until completely blended.

16. Leave the remaining batter white or add food coloring to it.

17. Pour the batters into a prepared cupcake tin that has been lightly floured and greased or lined with cupcake liners. You

will want to fill half of the cupcake tin with the white frosting and the other half with the chocolate.

18. Once the cupcake tins are ¾ of the way full, run a toothpick through the batter to create a marbled effect.

19. Bake at 350°F for 15 to 20 minutes or until a toothpick inserted in the middle of the cake comes out clean.

20. Remove and allow to cool in the tins for 10 minutes before placing them on a wire rack to cool completely.

Apple Pie Cupcakes

Many times we think of cupcakes as a cake and batter but you can mix up your cupcakes and make them from things besides cake. This apple pie cupcake is a great demonstration of that and is as delicious as a slice of warm apple pie.

Baking Tips, Tricks and Hints

Mint leaves can go well with any type of cupcake and make the perfect garnish. Always keep a few in your baking supplies to dress up any of your refrigerator cakes.

Ingredients:

Crust:

Dry:

- 1 cup of flour
- 1 tsp of white sugar
- Pinch of salt

Wet:

- 6 tbsp of butter, unsalted
- 2 tbsp of water

Filling:

Dry:

- 1/3 cup of white sugar

- 3 tsp of flour
- ¼ tsp of nutmeg
- ¾ tsp of cinnamon
- Pinch of salt

Wet:

- 3 large apples

Directions:

Crust:

1. In a large mixing bowl, sift the flour.
2. Add the butter and cut it into the flour with a pastry knife until it looks like crumbs.
3. Add the salt and mix.
4. Slowly add the water and mix until a soft dough begins to form. You may not need to use all of the water.
5. Place in the fridge and allow the dough to set for 20 minutes.
6. Remove from the fridge and roll out to a thin, ½ sheet.
7. Use a biscuit cutter and cut round biscuits from the dough.
8. Place the dough into a cupcake tin lined with cupcake liners. Make sure the dough is in the cupcake liner.
9. Fill with the apple filling.
10. Place a smaller circle of dough on the top.
11. Poke a few holes into the top with a fork and seal the edges by pressing the top and bottom together.
12. Place in the oven set at 375°F and bake for 20 to 30 minutes or until the crust begins to brown.
13. Remove from heat and allow to cool in the cupcake tin for 10 minutes before removing.
14. Cool completely before serving.

Filling:

1.	In a large mixing bowl, whisk together the sugar and flour.

2.	Add in the cinnamon, salt and nutmeg and mix until they are fully incorporated.

3.	Wash the apples.

4.	Peel, core and slice into small pieces that will fit into the cupcake tins.

5.	Place the apples into the dry ingredients.

6.	Toss until the apples are coated.

7.	Fill each cupcake with apple filling.

Chocolate Raspberry Surprise Cupcakes

This tasty little treat has everything you could ever want in a cupcake from the rich chocolate flavor to the tart raspberry touches. Sure to delight even the harshest of cupcake critics.

Baking Tips, Tricks and Hints

Whenever you have to melt any ingredients, melt them slowly on a low heat. Adding too much heat can burn or scald the ingredients and produce a negative flavor to your dish.

Ingredients:

Cupcakes:

Dry:

- 2 ½ cups of flour
- 3 cups of white sugar
- 2 tsp of baking soda
- ¾ tsp of baking powder
- 1 ¼ tsp of salt
- 1 ½ cups of cocoa powder, unsweetened
- 3 oz of semisweet chocolate

Wet:

- 1 ½ cups of buttermilk
- 1 ½ cups of coffee, hot
- ¾ tsp of vanilla
- ¾ cup of vegetable oil
- 3 eggs

Filling:

Dry:

- ¼ cup of sugar
- 1 tbsp of cornstarch

Wet:

- 1 ½ cups of frozen raspberries

Frosting:

Dry:

- 1 ½ tbsp of sugar
- 12 oz of semisweet chocolate

Wet:

- ¾ cup of heavy cream
- 3 tbsp of butter, unsalted
- 1 ½ tbsp of corn syrup

Directions:

Cupcake:

1. In a large mixing bowl, sift together the flour, baking soda, salt and baking powder.

2. Whisk in the sugar.

3. Whisk in the cocoa powder and mix until the dry ingredients are well blended.

4. Make a well in the center of the dry ingredients and set aside.

5. In a separate bowl, pour in the hot coffee. Make sure that it is hot and freshly brewed. If it is not really hot, warm it.

6. Chop up the chocolate and place the chocolate into the coffee. Let stand for a few minutes.

7. Once the chocolate is melted, mix the coffee mixture until it is smooth.

8. In a separate mixing bowl, whisk the eggs until they are thick and yellow.

9. Add the oil and blend completely.

10. Stir in the buttermilk and vanilla, again, mixing until they are fully incorporated.

11. Fold in the coffee mixture and mix completely.

12. Pour the egg mixture into the flour mixture.

13. Mix until the ingredients are moist. Do not over mix.

14. Pour into a prepared cupcake tin that has been lightly floured and greased or lined with cupcake liners.

15. Bake at 350°F for 15 to 20 minutes or until a toothpick inserted in the middle of the cake comes out clean.

16. Remove and allow to cool in the tins for 10 minutes before placing them on a wire rack to cool completely.

Filling:

1. In a food processer, puree the frozen raspberries.

2.   Strain through a sieve to remove the seeds and place the strained raspberries into a saucepan.

3.   Place on the stove and set the temperature to medium or medium low.

4.   Stir in the sugar.

5.   Whisk in the cornstarch.

6.   Bring the mixture to a boil, stirring frequently.

7.   Allow it to simmer for a few minutes until the mixture thickens.

8.   Remove from heat and allow to cool completely before using.

9.   Once it is chilled, place the filling into a pastry bag with an injecting tip on it.

10.   Press the tip into the cooled cupcake and pipe two to three teaspoons of filling into the center of the cupcake.

11.   Place the cupcakes into the fridge while you make the frosting.

Frosting:

1.   Chop the chocolate.

2.   Place it in a glass or heat proof bowl. Set aside.

3.   In a medium saucepan, whisk together the corn syrup and sugar.

4.   Pour in the cream and blend.

5.   Place the saucepan onto the stove and set to medium low heat.

6.   Bring the cream mixture to a slow boil, stirring constantly.

7.   Remove from heat and pour over the chocolate.

8.   Let stand until the chocolate melts.

9.   When it melts, blend until the mixture is smooth.

10.   Add the butter and mix until it has melted.

11. Pipe or spread onto the top of the filled cupcakes.

12. Decorate with raspberries.

Turned Upside Down Cupcakes

Upside down treats are not just for cakes and these little cupcakes are sure to turn your taste buds upside down as well. Perfect with a sweet topping, this recipe turns the everyday treat into something extraordinary.

Baking Tips, Tricks and Hints

When baking, always make sure that you read the recipe completely before you begin. This will prevent you from making a mistake while baking.

Ingredients:

Cupcakes:

Dry:

- 1 ¼ cups of flour
- 1 cup of white sugar
- ¼ tsp of baking soda
- ½ tsp of baking powder
- ¼ tsp of salt
- 1 ½ cups of pecans, chopped

Wet:

- ½ cup of sour cream
- 1 tsp of vanilla
- ½ cup of canola oil
- 1 egg

Topping:

Dry:

- 2/3 cup of brown sugar, packed

Wet:

- ½ cup of butter, unsalted
- 5 tbsp of honey

Directions:

Cupcakes:

1. In a large mixing bowl, sift together the baking powder, baking soda, salt and flour. Set aside.

2. Whisk together the egg and the sugar. Blend until it is thick and pale yellow.

3. Add in the oil and vanilla and mix until it is completely incorporated.

4. Fold in the sour cream. Mix completely.

5. Stir in the flour mixture and blend until the batter is smooth.

6. In a prepared cupcake tin that has been lightly floured and greased or lined with cupcake liners, add 1 ½ tsp of the topping to the bottom of the cupcake.

7. Place 2 tbsp of pecans on top of the topping.

8. Pour in the cupcake batter until the cupcake tins are ¾ of the way full.

9. Bake at 350°F for 20 to 25 minutes or until a toothpick inserted in the middle of the cake comes out clean.

10. Remove and allow to cool in the tins for 10 minutes before placing them on a wire rack to cool completely.

Topping:

1. In a medium saucepan set at medium-low heat, melt the butter.

2. Add the honey.

3. Stir in the brown sugar and continue to heat until the sugar melts, stir constantly.

4. Once melted, remove from heat and use as directed.

Oreo Cupcakes

Oreos are a favorite in my home all on their own but whenever I put them into a baked good, I get plenty of praise. There is no doubt that this cupcake will have everyone praising your baking ability and people will be asking you for seconds with this treat.

Baking Tips, Tricks and Hints

Whenever you make your own whipped cream, pour the cream into a cold bowl for the best results.

Ingredients:

Cupcakes:

Dry:

- 2 ½ cups of flour
- 1 2/3 cups of white sugar
- 1 tsp of baking powder
- ½ tsp of salt
- 24 Oreo halves with cream filling
- 20 Oreo Cookies

Wet:

- 8 tbsp of butter, unsalted
- 2 tsp of vanilla
- 1 cup of milk

- 2 eggs

Frosting:

Dry:

- 4 cups of icing sugar
- ½ cup of Oreo cookie crumbs
- 12 Oreo Cookies

Wet:

- 1 cup of cream cheese
- 1 tbsp of vanilla
- 2 tbsp of heavy cream
- 6 tbsp of butter, unsalted

Directions:

Cupcakes:

1. Separate 24 Oreo cookies so you only have one side of cookie and the cream instead of a full cookie.
2. Set aside.
3. In a medium mixing bowl, sift together the flour, salt and baking powder.
4. In a separate bowl, cream together the butter and sugar until it is light and fluffy.
5. Add an egg and blend completely.
6. Add the second egg and again, blend completely.
7. Fold in the vanilla and mix until the butter mixture is smooth.
8. Add half of the flour mixture and blend until it is incorporated. Do not over mix.
9. Pour in the milk and beat slightly, again, just until it is incorporated.

10. Fold in the remaining flour mixture, again, mix until it is just incorporated.

11. Chop up the 20 Oreo cookies.

12. Fold them into the cupcake batter until they are evenly dispersed. Never over mix.

13. Place the whole Oreo half, cream side facing up, into cupcake liners set in 2 cupcake tins. This recipe makes 24 cupcakes.

14. Pour the batter over top of the Oreo half until it is 2/3rds full.

    15. Bake at 350°F for 15 to 20 minutes or until a toothpick inserted in the middle of the cake comes out clean.

16. Remove and allow to cool in the tins for 10 minutes before placing them on a wire rack to cool completely.

Frosting:

1. In a large bowl, cream together the butter and cream cheese.

2. Add the vanilla and continue to blend until it is smooth.

3. Add in the icing sugar, a cup at a time, mixing until it is smooth each time.

4. Slowly add the heavy cream.

5. Whip the frosting for five minutes until you have a nice, light and fluffy frosting.

6. Pipe onto the cooled cupcakes.

7. Sprinkle with the Oreo cookie crumbs.

8. Cut the remaining Oreo cookies in half and garnish the cupcakes with the Oreo cookie.

The Vegan Recipes

Although the main focus of this section is to provide you with some wonderful cupcake recipes that are truly vegan, it is important to have a few basic vegan icing recipes to make sure your cupcake stays vegan. These recipes are wonderful treats and I find that they are often a big hit even with people who aren't vegan.

In this section, choose vegan alternatives for margarines, milks and ingredients that have been traditionally animal based.

I Dream of Applesauce Cupcakes

A sweetly divine cupcake, this recipe is perfect with vanilla frosting as a desert or even as a breakfast cupcake. The texture is delightful and the rich taste will make you dream of full orchards.

Baking Tips, Tricks and Hints

Use fresh, organic fruits for your vegan recipes. The end result will be a cupcake that tastes and looks magnificent.

Ingredients:

Dry:

- 1 ½ cups of flour
- ¼ cup of white sugar
- 1 tsp of baking soda
- ¼ tsp of salt
- 1 tsp of cinnamon, ground
- 1 ½ tsp of nutmeg, ground
- ¼ cup of chopped walnuts (optional)

Wet:

- ½ cup of non-dairy margarine
- 1 tsp of vanilla

- 1 ¼ cups of applesauce, unsweetened

Directions:

1. In a large mixing bowl, sift together the salt, baking soda and flour.

2. Add the cinnamon and nutmeg and whisk until the dry ingredients are fully incorporated.

3. Set aside.

4. In a separate mixing bowl, cream the margarine until it is light and fluffy.

5. Pour in the sugar and continue mixing until the margarine is smooth.

6. Pour a third of the dry ingredients into the margarine and sugar mixture. Mix thoroughly.

7. Fold in half of the applesauce. Mix completely.

8. Repeat the process, alternating between a third of the dry ingredients and half of the applesauce until you have incorporated all of the ingredients.

9. Fold in the vanilla and mix until the batter is smooth.

10. Add the nuts and gently blend until the nuts are dispersed through the batter.

11. Pour into a prepared cupcake tin that has been lightly floured and greased or lined with cupcake liners.

12. Bake at 350°F for 15 to 20 minutes or until a toothpick inserted in the middle of the cake comes out clean.

13. Remove and allow to cool in the tins for 10 minutes before placing them on a wire rack to cool completely.

Taste of Italy Cappuccino Cupcakes

Even if you can't get to Italy, you can still enjoy the flavors of Italy right at home. Definitely a treat for the adults in your life, this is an excellent cupcake to have for brunch or with a nice espresso.

Baking Tips, Tricks and Hints

An alternative to using eggs is to use half a banana mashed or a ¼ cup of applesauce. It changes the taste of the recipe slightly but not too much to notice.

Ingredients:

Dry:

- 2 cups of flour
- 1 ½ cups of white sugar
- 1 tsp of baking powder
- ½ tsp of salt
- ½ cup of cocoa powder, unsweetened
- ¼ cup of instant coffee

Wet:

- ½ cup of non-dairy margarine
- ¼ cup of vegetable oil
- ¼ cup of non-dairy yogurt
- ½ cup of warm water
- 2 tsp of vanilla
- ¼ cups of applesauce, unsweetened
- 1 ½ cups of non-dairy whipped cream

Directions:

1. Sift together the flour, baking soda and salt.

2. Whisk in the sugar.

3. Whisk in the cocoa powder and then set aside.

4. In a separate bowl, cream together the applesauce and margarine.

5. Fold in the oil and yogurt and mix until thoroughly blended.

6. Mix in the vanilla and stir until the ingredients are fully incorporated.

7. Add the instant coffee and mix until it is dissolved.

8. Pour in the dry ingredients and mix until the batter is smooth.

9. Pour into a prepared cupcake tin that has been lightly floured and greased or lined with cupcake liners.

10. Bake at 350°F for 15 to 20 minutes or until a toothpick inserted in the middle of the cake comes out clean.

11. Remove and allow to cool in the tins for 5 minutes before placing them on a wire rack to cool completely.

12. Top with whipped cream and dust lightly with cocoa powder.

Ginger Snaps Gingerbread Cupcakes

I love the taste of gingerbread but my biggest complaint is that most gingerbreads are just too hard. Gingerbread cupcakes on the other hand have the splendid taste of ginger with a nice soft cake that is perfect for a winter party.

Baking Tips, Tricks and Hints

To determine if your baking powder is still useable, add a small amount to boiling water. If it fizzes and bubbles up, it is still good.

Ingredients:

Dry:

- 1 ¼ cups of flour
- 2 cups of white sugar
- 1 tsp of baking soda
- ¼ tsp of salt
- ½ tsp of all spice, ground
- 3 tsp of cinnamon, ground
- 1 ½ tsp of ginger, ground
- ¼ tsp of cloves, ground
- 1 tbsp of crystallized ginger

Wet:

- 6 tbsp of non-dairy margarine
- 1 cup of vegan cream cheese
- ½ tsp of vanilla
- ¼ cups of applesauce, unsweetened
- ½ cup of molasses

Directions:

1. In a large mixing bowl, sift together the flour and salt.
2. Whisk in the 1 tsp of cinnamon.

3. Add in the allspice, cloves and ground ginger. Whisk until the dry ingredients are well blended.

4. In a separate bowl, cream together 4 tablespoons of margarine and ½ cup of sugar.

5. Cream until the ingredients become light and fluffy.

6. Add in the applesauce and mix until it is incorporated.

7. Fold in the molasses and mix until the sugar mixture is smooth.

8. Bring a half cup of water to a boil.

9. Stir in the baking soda until it has dissolved completely.

10. Pour the baking soda water into the sugar mixture.

11. Add the sugar mixture to the dry ingredients and blend until the batter is smooth.

12. Pour into a prepared cupcake tin that has been lightly floured and greased or lined with cupcake liners.

13. Bake at 350°F for 15 to 20 minutes or until a toothpick inserted in the middle of the cake comes out clean.

14. Remove and allow to cool in the tins for 5 minutes before placing them on a wire rack to cool completely.

15. While the cupcakes are baking, cream together the cream cheese, sugar and margarine until it is light and fluffy.

16. Fold in the cinnamon and vanilla and mix until it is smooth.

17. Place in the fridge and chill for at least 30 minutes.

18. Use the frosting to decorate the cooled cupcakes and then top with the crystallized ginger.

Snowy Mousse Cupcakes

Although we often think of mousse as being a milk chocolate pudding dessert, this completely vegan recipe brings mousse to the world of cupcakes, although simply with the liners, and provides a little twist by using white chocolate instead of dark or milk. Decadent while still being a cute crowd pleaser.

Baking Tips, Tricks and Hints

To create a nice texture to your cupcakes and to make them a little healthier, mix your flour. Use 1 part whole wheat and 1 part unbleached white flour. Only using whole wheat will make your cupcakes heavy and dry.

Ingredients:

Dry:

- 6 oz of non-dairy white chocolate
- 6 oz of vegan white chocolate

Wet:

- ¼ cup of applesauce
- ¼ cup of soy milk
- ¾ cup of non-dairy yogurt
- 4 oz of non-dairy whipped cream

Directions:

1.   In a double boiler, melt the non-dairy chocolate.   Make sure you only heat it until the chocolate is smooth.

2.   Once it is melted, line 6 cupcake tins with cupcake liners.

3.   Using a pastry brush, dip the brush into the melted chocolate.

4.   Brush the chocolate into each of the cupcake liners. Make sure you do the sides as well as the bottom of the cupcake liner.

5.   Place in the fridge for 10 minutes until the chocolate hardens.

6.   With the remaining melted chocolate, you may have to reheat the chocolate several times, brush on another 2 layers until you get a nice shell in the cupcake liners.

7.   Place in the freezer until you are ready to use them.

8.   While the shells are hardening, take the vegan white chocolate and melt it in the double boiler.

9.   Melt until the chocolate is smooth.

10. Remove from the heat and cool slightly.

11. In a separate mixing bowl, combine the yogurt and milk. Mix until well blended.

12. Add the applesauce and mix until the ingredients are smooth.

13. Fold a third of the applesauce mixture into the chocolate.

14. Fold in a third of the whipped cream.

15. Repeat until all of the whipped cream and applesauce mixture have been added to the chocolate.

16. Place in the fridge and allow them to cool completely, usually about 2 hours.

17. Remove from the fridge.

18. Carefully remove the chocolate shells from the cupcake liners.

19. Spoon the mousse into the chocolate shells.

20. Garnish with whipped cream and shaved chocolate.

21. Serve cold.

Whole Lotta Chips Chocolate Cupcakes

Chocolate chip cupcakes are a staple of any baker's recipe list much like chocolate chip cookies are. This treat is a wonderful cupcake that is moist, and has the perfect amount of chocolate chips all rolled into the perfect vegan recipe.

Baking Tips, Tricks and Hints

To make a well in dry ingredients, build a small hill with the ingredients and then press your thumb into the center of the hill to make a hole. Make sure the hole is large enough for the wet ingredients to be poured into it.

An alternative to using cupcake liners is to line the tins with parchment paper. It work just as well and you can simply pop the cupcake out of the pan and off of the paper to create the finished product.

Ingredients:

Dry:

- 1 ½ cups of flour
- 1 tsp of baking powder
- 1tsp of baking soda
- 1 cup of white sugar
- ½ tsp of salt
- 2 tbsp of cocoa powder, unsweetened
- ½ cup of non dairy chocolate chips

Wet:

- ¼ cup of canola oil
- ½ cup of warm water
- 1 tsp of vanilla
- 1 tbsp of apple cider vinegar

Directions:

1. In a large mixing bowl, sift together the baking powder, flour, baking soda and salt.

2.   Whisk in the sugar and cocoa powder until it is well blended.

3.   Make a well in the middle of the dry ingredients.

4.   In a separate bowl, mix together the oil and vanilla.

5.   Fold in the vinegar.

6.   Stir in the warm water and mix until the wet ingredients are well blended.

7.   Pour the wet ingredients into the well you made.

8.   Blend until the batter is moist. Do not over mix.

9.   Pour into a prepared cupcake tin that has been lightly floured and greased or lined with cupcake liners.

10. Bake at 400°F for 15 to 20 minutes or until a toothpick inserted in the middle of the cake comes out clean.

11. Remove and allow to cool in the tins for 5 minutes before placing them on a wire rack to cool completely.

Orange Surprise Cupcakes

This is a fun little recipe that has a wonderful, moist cake and in the center is an orange goo that surprises as much as its flavor delights. Perfect with many different types of coffee, this cupcake is a popular hit with most grownups and many kids too.

Baking Tips, Tricks and Hints

An alternative to using cupcake liners is to line the tins with parchment paper. It work just as well and you can simply pop the cupcake out of the pan and off of the paper to create the finished product.

Ingredients:

Cupcake:

Dry:

- 3 cups of flour
- 2 tsp of baking soda
- ½ tsp of salt
- ½ cup of cocoa powder, unsweetened
- 2 cups of white sugar

Wet:

- ½ cup of vegetable oil
- 2 tbsp of vegetable oil
- 2 tsp of vanilla
- 2 cups of water
- 2 tbsp of apple cider vinegar

Filling:

Dry:

- 1/3 cup of white sugar
- 6 oz of non dairy chocolate chips

Wet:

- 1 cup of vegan cream cheese
- ¼ cup of non-dairy yogurt
- Yellow Food Coloring
- Red Food Coloring

Directions:

Cupcake:

1.   In a large mixing bowl, sift together the flour, baking soda and salt.

2.   Whisk in the sugar and cocoa powder.

3.   Create a well in the center of the dry ingredients and set aside.

4.   In a separate bowl, whisk together the vegetable oil and vanilla.

5.   Add in the vinegar and mix until they are well blended.

6.   Pour in the water and blend until the ingredients are mixed thoroughly.

7.   Pour the wet ingredients into the well and mix until the ingredients are moist. Do not over mix.

8.   Pour the batter into the prepared cupcake tin that has been lightly floured and greased or lined with cupcake liners. You only want to fill the cupcake liners half way.

9.   Spoon 1 teaspoon of the filling into the center of the cupcake batter in each liner.

10. Bake at 350°F for 20 to 25 minutes in a preheated oven or until a toothpick inserted in the middle of the cake comes out clean.

11. Remove and allow to cool in the tins for 5 minutes before placing them on a wire rack to cool completely.

Filling:

1.   In a large mixing bowl, cream together the cream cheese and yogurt.

2.   Fold in the sugar and mix until the ingredients are smooth.

3.   Add in the food coloring to create the desired shade of orange.

4.   Fold in the chocolate chips.

5.   Set Aside.

Lavender Garden Cupcakes

A grown up taste in a childlike dessert, these are wonderful cupcakes for an afternoon tea since they have a rich floral taste to them. The lavender taste is an excellent compliment to any meal or tea.

Baking Tips, Tricks and Hints

Always preheat your oven before you start baking. If you don't, foods can be undercooked or burnt very easily.

Ingredients:

Dry:

- 1 ¼ cups of flour
- ½ tsp of baking soda
- ¾ tsp of baking powder
- ¼ tsp of salt
- 1 tbsp of cornstarch
- 2 tsp of dried lavender flowers
- ¾ cup of white sugar

Wet:

- ¼ cup of vegan margarine
- ½ cup of non dairy milk
- 1 tsp of lemon extract
- 4 oz of sweet potato baby food

Directions:

1. Finely chop the lavender flowers and set to the side.

2. In a large mixing bowl, cream together the margarine and sugar.

3. Mix until it is light and fluffy.

4. Fold in the sweet potato baby food. Mix until smooth.

5. In a small bowl, whisk together the cornstarch and milk.

6. Pour into the sugar mixture and blend until the ingredients are smooth.

7. In a separate bowl, sift together the baking powder, baking soda, flour and salt.

8. Slowly add the flour mixture to the sugar mixture.

9. Stir until the ingredients are smooth.

10. Mix in the lemon extract.

11. Fold in the lavender flowers.

12. Pour into a prepared cupcake tin that has been lightly floured and greased or lined with cupcake liners.

13. Bake at 350°F for 15 to 20 minutes or until a toothpick inserted in the middle of the cake comes out clean.

14. Remove and allow to cool in the tins for 5 minutes before placing them on a wire rack to cool completely.

15. Decorate with frosting and garnish with fresh lavender flowers.

What's Up Doc? Carrot Cupcakes

Another favorite wherever you go, carrot cupcakes are a great way to enjoy a classic treat without having to make a huge cake.

Baking Tips, Tricks and Hints

When decorating cupcakes, make your own colored sprinkles by adding a few drops of food coloring to granulated sugar. Shake until the sugar is coated.

Ingredients:

Dry:

- 1 ¾ cups of flour
- 1 tsp of baking soda
- 2 tsp of baking powder
- ¾ tsp of salt
- ½ tsp of nutmeg, ground
- 1 ½ tsp of cinnamon, ground
- 1 ½ cups of white sugar
- ½ cup of brown sugar
- ½ cup of walnuts, chopped
- ½ cup of non-dairy chocolate chips

Wet:

- 1 cup of vegetable oil
- ½ cup of non dairy yogurt

- 1 tsp of vanilla
- ½ cup of applesauce
- 2 tbsp of orange juice
- 3 cups of carrots, grated

Directions:

1. Wash and peel the carrots.

2. Grate the carrots and set aside.

3. In a large mixing bowl, sift together the baking powder, baking soda, salt and flour.

4. Whisk in the cinnamon and nutmeg.

5. In a separate bowl, blend together the applesauce and yogurt.

6. Mix until the ingredients are smooth.

7. Fold in the sugar.

8. Add the vanilla and continue to mix.

9. Mix in the vegetable oil and orange juice.

10. Blend until the ingredients are smooth.

11. Pour a third of the dry ingredients into the wet ingredients.

12. Mix until it is smooth.

13. Repeat the process, mixing in only a third of the dry ingredients and blend until it is completely blended until all of the ingredients are incorporated.

14. Fold in the grated carrots.

15. Add in the chocolate chips and walnuts.

16. Stir until they are fully dispersed throughout the batter.

17. Pour into a prepared cupcake tin that has been lightly floured and greased or lined with cupcake liners.

18. Bake at 350°F for 15 to 20 minutes or until a toothpick inserted in the middle of the cake comes out clean.

19. Remove and allow to cool in the tins for 5 minutes before placing them on a wire rack to cool completely.

Cherries Jubilee Cupcakes

The perfect summer dessert, this recipe is full of cherry goodness and has a unique blend of sweet sugars and tart cherries.

Baking Tips, Tricks and Hints

Vegan batters are usually very moist and you may need to add a small amount of extra flour to create a better batter.

Ingredients:

Dry:

- 1 ¾ cups of flour
- 1 tsp of baking soda
- 1 cup of white sugar
- 3 tbsp of white sugar
- ½ cup of walnuts, chopped

Wet:

- ½ cup of vegetable oil
- ¼ cup of non dairy yogurt
- ½ tsp of almond extract
- ¼ cup of applesauce

- 1 cup of cherries, crushed

Directions:

1. Wash and pit the cherries.

2. In a mixing bowl, crush the cherries.

3. Stir in the 3 tablespoons of sugar.

4. Cover and place in the fridge.

5. In a separate bowl, sift together the baking soda and flour.

6. Whisk in the sugar until the ingredients are well blended.

7. Fold in the nuts. Set aside.

8. In a large mixing bowl, cream together the applesauce and yogurt.

9. Add the almond extract and mix until incorporated.

10. Stir in the oil and continue to mix until the ingredients are smooth.

11. Fold in the cherries and continue to mix until the cherries are broken.

12. Combine the wet and dry ingredients and mix until smooth.

13. Pour into a prepared cupcake tin that has been lightly floured and greased or lined with cupcake liners.

14. Bake at 350˚F for 15 to 20 minutes or until a toothpick inserted in the middle of the cake comes out clean.

15. Remove and allow to cool in the tins for 5 minutes before placing them on a wire rack to cool completely.

Touch of Mint Cupcakes

Mint is always refreshing and you won't be disappointed with this non bake cupcake. The refreshing taste has the right amount of mint and the rich chocolate only emphasises how perfect the mint is.

Baking Tips, Tricks and Hints

When you are baking vegan recipes, it is often recommended to set your oven to about 25°F above the recommended temperature since there is often more moisture to bake out of the batter.

Ingredients:

Dry:

- 2 cups of white sugar
- 6 oz of non dairy chocolate chips
- ¼ cup of chopped walnuts

Wet:

- 1 cup of vegan margarine
- ½ cup of non dairy yogurt
- ¼ cup of applesauce
- 1 tsp of vanilla
- 1 tsp of peppermint extract
- ¼ cup of tofu, silken

Directions:

1. In a double boiler, melt the chocolate chips. Set aside and allow to cool slightly.

2.   In a separate bowl, cream the margarine and sugar together until smooth.

3.   Fold in the chocolate. Mix on high for about 5 minutes.

4.   Add in the applesauce and yogurt, blend until smooth.

5.   Fold in the tofu and continue mixing.

6.   Add the vanilla.

7.   Stir in the peppermint extract and mix until all the ingredients are incorporated.

8.   Place cupcake liners in 24 cupcake tins.

9.   Pour a thin layer of walnuts over the bottom of each liner.

10. Spoon the mint mixture over the nuts until the liner is ¾ full.

11.   Garnish with the remaining nuts.

12. Place in the fridge and allow to set for two hours.

13. Serve cold.

Vegan Vanilla Frosting

Although the many cupcake recipes in this book are perfect just on their own, this vanilla frosting will not only dress up your cupcakes but provide them with an extra element full of taste.

Baking Tips, Tricks and Hints

Always sift your icing sugar when you are making frosting for a nicer consistency.

Ingredients:

Dry:

- 3 cups of icing sugar

Wet:

- ½ cup of vegan margarine
- ¼ cup of non dairy milk
- 1 tbsp of vanilla

Directions:

1. In a large mixing bowl, cream together the margarine and vanilla.

2. Slowly add the milk and mix until the ingredients are smooth.

3. Add a half cup of the icing sugar and blend completely.

4. Repeat, adding a half cup of icing sugar and mixing completely each time.

5. Finish with the remaining icing sugar and mix until smooth and creamy.

6. Add food coloring to create the desired shade or use as white.

Vegan Chocolate Frosting

You can't have cupcakes without having a really good chocolate frosting and it can be difficult to find that when you are looking for a vegan alternative. Well this frosting proves that you don't have to sacrifice when it comes to eating vegan and enjoying chocolate.

Baking Tips, Tricks and Hints

When you are baking vegan, make sure you avoid products that have whey in them since these are animal based. Many vegan products contain whey so make sure the ones you choose do not.

Ingredients:

Dry:

*   4 cups of icing sugar
*   ¼ cup of cocoa powder, unsweetened
*   Dash of salt

Wet:

*   6 oz of non-dairy cream cheese
*   ½ cup of non dairy chocolate milk

- 1 tbsp of vanilla

Directions:

1. In a large mixing bowl, cream together the cocoa powder and cream cheese.

2. Add in the milk and mix until the ingredients are smooth.

3. Add a half cup of the icing sugar and blend completely.

4. Repeat, adding a half cup of icing sugar and mixing completely each time.

5. Finish with the remaining icing sugar and mix until smooth and creamy.

Vegan Buttercream Frosting

Buttercream is a very rich icing that has a creamy texture to it, which hardens slightly after setting. Perfect with a range of cupcakes, this is a nice frosting to decorate with as well.

Baking Tips, Tricks and Hints

When decorating cupcakes, use different tips for decorating.

Ingredients:

Dry:

- 3 cups of icing sugar
- ¼ cup of cocoa powder, unsweetened
- Dash of salt

Wet:

- ½ cup of vegan margarine
- ¼ cup of non dairy milk
- 1 tbsp of vanilla

Directions:

1. In a large mixing bowl, cream together the margarine and vanilla.

2. Add in the milk and mix until the ingredients are smooth.

3. Add a half cup of the icing sugar and blend completely.

4. Repeat, adding a half cup of icing sugar and mixing completely each time.

5. Finish with the remaining icing sugar and mix until smooth and creamy.

6. Color with food coloring.

Vegan Cream Cheese Frosting

The final vegan frosting is a popular one for most bakers and it is perfect for carrot cake and other cupcakes. This frosting is very easy to make and even easier to decorate with. This recipe can be made with the spices for a twist on a classic recipe or without to make the more traditional cream cheese frosting.

Baking Tips, Tricks and Hints

Never over mix will your ingredients or you find the consistency is not as light and airy as you would like.

Ingredients:

Dry:

- 1 ½ cups of icing sugar
- ¼ tsp of nutmeg, ground
- 2 tsp of cinnamon, ground
- 1 tsp of ginger, ground

Wet:

- 1 cup of non-dairy cream cheese
- 2 tbsp of vegan margarine

Directions:

1. In a large mixing bowl, cream together the cream cheese and margarine until it is light and fluffy.

2. Add in the vanilla and continue to blend until it is smooth.

3. In a separate bowl, whisk together the spices and sugar.

4. Slowly add the sugar mixture to the cream cheese mixture, stirring as you do.

5. Continue to blend until the mixture is light and fluffy.

6. Chill before using for about 30 minutes.

The Low Fat Recipes

When it comes to delicious cupcakes, everyone enjoys having a cupcake, even if your diet screams at you to avoid them. Well, these recipes will not only take away the guilt of having a cupcake but they will also take away the worry since they are a healthy choice to the more decadent cakes out there.

Chocolate Fudge Cupcakes

The must have recipe for anyone who loves chocolate but wants to keep to their diet – this treat will meet all your expectations and then some. A perfect blend of chocolate, the cupcake is easy to make and even easier to eat.

Baking Tips, Tricks and Hints

If you are making smaller batches of chocolate, melt the chocolate in a microwave. Set the time for short 30 second intervals and stir every time you reset the timer. Never overheat chocolate or it will go dry and unpalatable.

Ingredients:

Dry:

- 1 ½ cups of flour
- 1 tsp of baking soda

- ¾ cup of sugar
- ½ tsp of salt
- ¼ cup of cocoa powder, unsweetened
- 1/3 cup of semisweet chocolate chips

Wet:

- 2 tbsp of butter
- ½ cup of buttermilk
- 1/3 cup of water
- 1 tsp of vanilla
- 2 eggs
- 1 tbsp of white vinegar

Directions:

1. In a large mixing bowl, cream together the butter and sugar until it is light and fluffy.

2. Set aside.

3. Take one egg and separate the egg white from the egg yolk. Throw away the egg yolk from one egg.

4. Add the egg white to the butter mixture. Blend until smooth.

5. Add the remaining egg to the butter mixture. Blend.

6. Mix in the buttermilk and water.

7. Add the vanilla and mix until fully incorporated.

8. Mix the vinegar into the wet ingredients and mix until smooth.

9. In a separate bowl, sift together the flour, baking soda and salt.

10. Whisk in the cocoa powder.

11. Make a well in the ingredients and pour the wet ingredients into it.

12. Blend until the batter is moist but do not over mix.

13. Fold in the chocolate chips and mix until they are dispersed through the batter.

14. Pour into a prepared cupcake tin that has been lightly floured and greased or lined with cupcake liners.

15. Bake at 375°F for 15 to 20 minutes or until a toothpick inserted in the middle of the cake comes out clean.

16. Remove and allow to cool in the tins for 10 minutes before placing them on a wire rack to cool completely.

17. Top with chocolate frosting.

Pineapple Delight Cupcake

Sweetness doesn't have to come from sugar and you can easily have a nice, light and insanely sweet treat when you make this pineapple cupcake.

Baking Tips, Tricks and Hints

The best way to zest a lemon for recipes is by using a microplane grater. The result is lemon zest that has practically no pith, which can affect your recipe

Ingredients:

Dry:

- 1 cup of flour
- 1 tsp of baking soda
- 1 cup of white sugar
- 3 tbsp of icing sugar

Wet:

- ¾ tsp of vanilla
- 10 oz of pineapple, crushed
- 3 egg whites

Directions:

1. In a large mixing bowl, sift together the flour and baking soda.

2. Whisk in the white sugar and set aside.

3. In a separate bowl, add the pineapple and vanilla. Mix until it is well blended.

4. Separate the egg whites and yolks from your eggs. Throw away the egg yolks and add the egg whites to the pineapple.

5. Mix until it is thoroughly mixed.

6. Add the pineapple mixture to the dry ingredients.

7. Mix until the batter is well blended.

8. Pour into a prepared cupcake tin that has been lightly floured and greased or lined with cupcake liners.

9. Bake at 350°F for 20 to 25 minutes or until a toothpick inserted in the middle of the cake comes out clean.

10. Remove and allow to cool in the tins for 10 minutes before placing them on a wire rack to cool completely.

11. Once they are cooled, dust them with the icing sugar and serve.

Warm and Inviting Pumpkin Cupcakes

Pumpkin and spice and everything nice are the perfect way to describe these mouth watering cupcakes. They are perfect for any season and won't play havoc with your waistline as much as other cupcakes.

Baking Tips, Tricks and Hints

Most cupcakes can be stored in the freezer for up to 3 months, just make sure they are in an airtight container.

Ingredients:

Dry:

- 2 2/3 cup of flour
- 1 tbsp of baking powder
- ½ tsp of nutmeg, ground
- 1 tsp of ginger, ground
- ½ tsp of cloves, ground
- Pinch of salt
- 1/3 cup of brown sugar, packed
- 3 tbsp of candied ginger
- 4 tbsp of pumpkin seeds

Wet:

- ¾ cup of fat free milk
- ½ cup of pureed pumpkin

- 1/3 cup of sunflower oil
- 10 oz of pineapple, crushed
- 1 egg

Directions:

1. In a mixing bowl, sift together the flour, baking powder and salt.

2. Whisk in the cinnamon, cloves and nutmeg.

3. Stir in the brown sugar.

4. Make a well in the dry ingredients and set to the side.

5. In a separate bowl, cream together the milk and oil.

6. Add in the egg and mix until well blended.

7. Fold in pumpkin and continue to mix until the ingredients are fully incorporated.

8. Pour the pumpkin mixture into the well of dry ingredients. Mix until the ingredients are moist but do not over mix.

9. Fold in the candied ginger.

10. Pour into a prepared cupcake tin that has been lightly floured and greased or lined with cupcake liners.

11. Sprinkle the pumpkin seeds onto all of the cupcakes.

12. Bake at 350°F for 20 to 25 minutes or until a toothpick inserted in the middle of the cake comes out clean.

13. Remove and allow to cool in the tins for 10 minutes before placing them on a wire rack to cool completely.

Basic Low Fat Chocolate Cupcakes

Sometimes getting back to basics is the best way to enjoy baking and everyone is sure to enjoy these low fat chocolate cupcakes that are as nice to the waistline as they are to the taste buds.

Baking Tips, Tricks and Hints

To determine if your baking powder is still useable, add a small amount to boiling water. If it fizzes and bubbles up, it is still good.

Ingredients:

Dry:

- 1 1/3 cups of flour
- ¾ cup of brown sugar, packed
- 1 ½ tsp of baking powder
- 1 ½ tsp of baking soda
- 2 tsp of salt
- ½ cup of cocoa powder, unsweetened

Wet:

- 2/3 cup of fat free milk
- ¼ cup of applesauce
- 1 tsp of vanilla
- 1 tbsp of vegetable oil
- 3 egg whites

Directions:

1.   Sift together the salt, flour, baking soda and baking powder.

2.   Whisk in the cocoa powder and set aside.

3.   In a separate bowl, cream together the sugar and applesauce.

4.   Stir in the vanilla and the vegetable oil and mix until well blended.

5.   Separate your egg yolks and egg whites. Throw away the egg yolks.

6.   Fold the egg whites into your sugar mixture.

7.   Add 1/3 of the flour mixture to the sugar mixture. Blend until moist.

8.   Add 1/3 of the milk to the sugar mix, blend until the ingredients are smooth.

9.   Repeat, alternating milk and flour, until all of the ingredients have been incorporated.

10. Pour into a prepared cupcake tin that has been lightly floured and greased or lined with cupcake liners.

11. Bake at 350°F for 20 to 25 minutes or until a toothpick inserted in the middle of the cake comes out clean.

12. Remove and allow to cool in the tins for 10 minutes before placing them on a wire rack to cool completely.

Coconut Symphony Cupcakes

Coconut sweetness abounds in this wonderful cupcake featuring its own glaze. The cupcake provides a symphony of taste in a small package that will become a popular treat all year round.

Baking Tips, Tricks and Hints

Sweeten your own fresh coconut for a fresh taste by cooking it in a syrup of 1 part water and 1 part sugar. Simmer for 15 minutes, let it set overnight and then drain the coconut, allow the coconut to dry before using.

Ingredients:

Cupcake:

Dry:

- 2 ½ cups of flour
- 2 cups of white sugar
- 2 tsp of baking soda
- ½ tsp of salt
- 2/3 cup of cocoa powder, unsweetened

Wet:

- 2 ¼ cups of fat free milk
- 6 tbsp of applesauce, unsweetened
- 1 tsp of vanilla

Filling:

Dry:

- 1 cup of flaked coconut
- 2 tbsp of cornstarch
- 2 tbsp of white sugar

Wet:

- 1 cup of light soy milk

Directions:

Filling:

1. In a medium saucepan, stir together the milk and cornstarch.

2. Add in the sugar and mix completely.

3. Set the temperature on the stove for medium-low.

4. Bring the milk to a boil, stirring constantly.

5. Remove from heat and allow to cool for 5 minutes.

6. Fold in the coconut.

7. Cover and place in the fridge to set for an hour.

Cupcake:

1. In a large mixing bowl, sift together the baking soda, flour and salt.

2. Whisk in the cocoa powder and sugar.

3. Mix until well blended.

4. Make a well in the dry ingredients and set aside.

5. In a separate bowl, blend together the applesauce and milk.

6. Fold in the vanilla extract and mix until thoroughly incorporated.

7. Pour the applesauce mixture into the flour mixture well.

8. Mix until the batter is smooth.

9. Pour into a prepared cupcake tin that has been lightly floured and greased or lined with cupcake liners. Make sure they are only half full.

10. Spoon a teaspoon of the coconut filling into the center of each cupcake.

11. Add another teaspoon of batter to cover the filling.

12. Bake at 350°F for 25 to 30 minutes or until a toothpick inserted in the middle of the cake comes out clean.

13. Remove and allow to cool in the tins for 10 minutes before placing them on a wire rack to cool completely.

Fall Apples Cupcakes

Every fall, I take the time to go out to the apple orchards and pick some apples. There is nothing more enjoyable on a warm fall day and this recipe often reminds me of those special moments. Although it uses applesauce instead of apples, this recipe will bring that fall orchard to mind while keeping those calories off your hips.

Baking Tips, Tricks and Hints

To separate egg whites from egg yolks, wash your hands and then place the egg in your hand, allow the egg white to run between your fingers to the bowl and switch the yolk from hand to hand gently pressing the egg white away from the yolk.

Ingredients:

Dry:

- 1 ½ cups of flour
- ¼ cup of white sugar
- 1 tsp of baking soda
- ¼ tsp of salt
- 1 tsp of cinnamon, ground
- 1 ½ tsp of nutmeg, ground
- ¼ cup of walnuts, chopped

Wet:

- ½ cup of low fat margarine
- 1 cup of applesauce, unsweetened
- 1 tsp of vanilla
- 1 egg

Directions:

1. In a large mixing bowl, sift together the flour, salt, and baking soda. Set aside.

2. In a separate bowl, cream together the margarine and sugar until it is light and fluffy.

3. Add the egg and mix until well blended.

4. Fold in the flour mixture and mix until smooth.

5. Add the applesauce and vanilla and blend.

6. Fold in the nuts and continue mixing until the nuts are thoroughly dispersed through the batter.

7. Pour into a prepared cupcake tin that has been lightly floured and greased or lined with cupcake liners.

8. Bake at 375°F for 15 to 20 minutes or until a toothpick inserted in the middle of the cake comes out clean.

9. Remove and allow to cool in the tins for 10 minutes before placing them on a wire rack to cool completely.

Strawberry Dream Cupcakes

Spring is a popular time for strawberries but this low fat cupcake will prove to anyone that strawberries can be enjoyed year round.

Baking Tips, Tricks and Hints

Always use fresh spices when you bake. If the spices are over 6 months old, you should purchase new ones.

Ingredients:

Dry:

- 1 cup of wheat flour
- 1 cup of whole grain flour
- 1 cup of brown sugar, packed
- 2 tbsp of brown sugar
- 1 tsp of baking powder
- ½ tsp of baking soda
- ½ tsp of salt
- ½ tsp of cardamom powder
- 12 strawberries

Wet:

- ½ cup of low fat milk
- 3 tbsp of light olive oil
- 2 tsp of vanilla
- 1 egg white

Directions:

1. In a large mixing bowl, sift together the flours, salt, baking powder and baking soda.

2. Whisk in the cardamom powder.

3. Make a well in the dry ingredients and set aside.

4. In a separate bowl, cream together the 1 cup of sugar and oil.

5. Separate the egg white from the egg yolk and throw away the egg yolk.

6. Pour the egg white into the sugar mixture and mix until well blended.

7. Continue to mix until the sugar mixture is light and fluffy, usually takes one minute on high.

8. Slowly add the milk and continue to mix.

9. Fold in the vanilla and mix until incorporated.

10. Pour the wet ingredients into the well of dry ingredients.

11. Mix until smooth.

12. Wash the strawberries.

13. Slice 8 of them into thin slices and place in a small bowl.

14. Add the 2 tbsp of sugar and toss until the strawberries are coated.

15. Lay the strawberries into each of the cupcake liners.

16. Pour the batter over the strawberries until the liner is ¾ full.

17. Bake at 350°F for 15 to 20 minutes or until a toothpick inserted in the middle of the cake comes out clean.

18. Remove and allow to cool in the tins for 10 minutes before placing them on a wire rack to cool completely.

19. Garnish with the remaining strawberries.

Simple Low Fat Vanilla Cupcakes

Fresh taste always abounds in the simplest things and these cupcakes are sure to please any critic, especially the ones that are looking for a low fat treat.

Baking Tips, Tricks and Hints

To keep baking low fat, substitute fruit for your sugar. A small amount of fruit can half the amount of sugar that you place in the recipe. By following this tip, you can make any recipe low fat.

Ingredients:
Dry:

- 1 1/3 cup of flour
- 1 cup of white sugar
- ½ tsp of baking powder
- ½ tsp of baking soda
- ¼ tsp of salt

Wet:

- 1 cup of low fat buttermilk
- ¼ cup of low fat margarine
- 1 tsp of vanilla
- 1 egg

Directions:

1.   In a medium mixing bowl, sift together the flour, baking soda, baking powder and salt. Set aside.

2.   In a separate bowl, cream together the margarine and sugar until it is light and fluffy.

3.   Add the egg and mix until the mixture is smooth.

4.   Fold in the vanilla and blend thoroughly.

5.   Slowly pour in half of the flour mixture and mix until combined.

6.   Add half of the buttermilk, again, mixing until combined.

7.   Pour in the remaining flour and mix until combined.

8.   Add the remaining buttermilk and mix until smooth.

9.   Pour into a prepared cupcake tin that has been lightly floured and greased or lined with cupcake liners.

10.   Bake at 350°F for 15 to 20 minutes or until a toothpick inserted in the middle of the cake comes out clean.

11.   Remove and allow to cool in the tins for 10 minutes before placing them on a wire rack to cool completely.

Peanut Butter and Chocolate Cup Cupcakes

For most of us, chocolate and peanut butter are not something that we think of with low fat but this recipe, with cupcakes (including the icing) only being 200 calories each, is sure to fit into any diet.

Baking Tips, Tricks and Hints

When baking cakes, make sure you sift the flour more than once for the best results.

Ingredients:

Cupcake

Dry:

- 1 ¾ cups of flour
- 1 cup of sugar substitute
- 1 cup of brown sugar, packed
- 1 ½ tsp of baking powder
- 1 ½ tsp of baking soda
- 1 tsp of salt
- ¾ cup of cocoa powder, unsweetened

Wet:

- 1 ¼ cup of low fat buttermilk
- ¼ cup of canola oil
- 2 tsp of vanilla
- 2 eggs
- 1 cup of hot coffee

Frosting:

Dry:

- 1 cups of icing sugar
- 2 tbsp of peanuts, chopped

Wet:

- ¼ cup of peanut butter
- ¼ cup of fat free ricotta cheese
- ½ tsp of vanilla
- ¼ cup of fat free cream cheese

Directions:

Cupcakes:

1.   In a large bowl, sift together the flour, baking soda, baking powder and salt.

2.   Whisk in the cocoa powder and mix until well blended.

3.   Whisk in the white sugar, again, mixing until thoroughly incorporated.

4.   Make a well in the dry ingredients and set aside.

5.   In a separate bowl, mix together the oil and brown sugar.

6.   Pour in the buttermilk and mix until smooth.

7.   Add the vanilla.

8.   Make a cup of black, hot coffee.

9.   Pour into the buttermilk mixture and blend until full incorporated.

10.   Pour the wet ingredients into the well of dry ingredients.

11.   Mix until the batter is smooth.

12.   Pour into a prepared cupcake tin that has been lightly floured and greased or lined with cupcake liners.

13.   Bake at 350°F for 20 to 25 minutes or until a toothpick inserted in the middle of the cake comes out clean.

14.   Remove and allow to cool in the tins for 10 minutes before placing them on a wire rack to cool completely.

Frosting:

1.   In a large mixing bowl, cream together the peanut butter and cream cheese.

2.   Add the ricotta cheese and blend until smooth.

3.   Fold in the vanilla and mix until well blended.

4.   Pour in a half cup of icing sugar, mix completely.

5.   Repeat with the remaining icing sugar and mix until the frosting is smooth.

6. Frost the cooled cupcakes and top with the chopped peanuts.

Yellow Mellow Lemon Cupcakes

The first time you taste these wonderful little cupcakes, you will be wondering if you are breaking your diet. Thankfully, these sweet little morsels are low in fat and perfect for an afternoon of decadence that won't break your diet.

Baking Tips, Tricks and Hints

To prevent your baking from becoming discolored, use white vanilla extract. The taste is the same but you won't have any discoloration.

Ingredients:
Dry:
- 1 ½ cups of flour
- 1 cup of sugar substitute
- ¾ tsp of baking soda
- ¼ tsp of salt

Wet:
- ¾ cup of low fat sour cream
- ¼ cup of low fat butter
- ½ tsp of vanilla

- 2 egg whites
- Lemon Zest
- 1 tbsp of lemon juice

Directions:

1.   In a mixing bowl, sift together the flour, salt and baking soda. Set aside.

2.   In a separate bowl, cream together the butter and sugar until it is light and fluffy.

3.   Separate the egg whites from the egg yolks and throw out the egg yolks.

4.   Add the egg whites to the butter mixture and blend until the mixture is creamy.

5.   Squeeze a fresh lemon and zest it.

6.   Add the zest to the butter mixture, mix completely.

7.   In a separate bowl, blend together the lemon juice and sour cream.

8.   Pour the sour cream into the butter mixture, blend until well mixed.

9.   Add the flour mixture to the butter mixture, mix until the batter is light and fluffy.

10. Pour into a prepared cupcake tin that has been lightly floured and greased or lined with cupcake liners.

11. Bake at 350°F for 15 to 20 minutes or until a toothpick inserted in the middle of the cake comes out clean.

12. Remove and allow to cool in the tins for 10 minutes before placing them on a wire rack to cool completely.

Low Fat Chocolate Glaze

When you are eating healthy, it is important to have a few low fat choices for your frostings and glazes. This chocolate glaze is very easy to make and the low calories will keep you from feeling any guilt from this pleasure.

Baking Tips, Tricks and Hints

A great way to cut down on the calories is to substitute chocolate with unsweetened cocoa powder; this will give you the same flavor with fewer calories.

Ingredients:

Dry:

- ½ cups of icing sugar
- 1 tbsp of cocoa powder, unsweetened
- Pinch of salt

Wet:

- ¼ tsp of vanilla
- 1 tbsp of boiling water
- 1 tbsp of low fat milk

Directions:

1. In a small mixing bowl, whisk together the icing sugar and the cocoa powder.

2. Add the pinch of salt and blend until the ingredients are fully incorporated.

3. Fold in the vanilla and mix until blended.

4. Add the boiling water and mix until the glaze is smooth.

5. Slowly add in the milk until you have a thin consistency. You may not have to use all of the milk.

6. Using a spoon, dribble the glaze over your cupcakes.

7. Place in the fridge before serving.

Skinny Vanilla Frosting

Vanilla icing can go with just about any cupcake and this light frosting is low fat and really makes for an excellent topping for any cupcake or cake treat.

Baking Tips, Tricks and Hints

Substitute whole milks or creams by using low fat buttermilk. There is less fat but it still provides the same consistency you need for the recipe.

Ingredients:
Dry:

- 2 cups of icing sugar

Wet:

- ¼ cup of low fat butter
- 1 tbsp of boiling water
- 1 tsp of vanilla

Directions:

1. In a large mixing bowl, cream together the vanilla and butter.

2. Add in the icing sugar, a half cup at a time, and blend completely between each one.

3. When the icing sugar is incorporated, slowly add the boiling water until you get a creamy texture. You may not have to use all of the water.

4. Use the icing to frost your cupcakes.

Chocolate Whipped Frosting

Although I have included a glaze, there is nothing as decadent as a chocolate frosting and even if you are counting your calories, there is no reason why you can't enjoy a low fat option to a classic.

Baking Tips, Tricks and Hints

Always use egg whites in your baking instead of full eggs to cut down on the calories. Be aware that you may need to add one additional egg white to accommodate the loss of each yolk.

Ingredients:

Dry:

- 1 1/3 cups of icing sugar
- 1/3 cup of cocoa powder, unsweetened

Wet:

- ¼ cup of skim milk
- ½ tsp of vanilla
- ¼ cup of fat free sour cream

Directions:

1. In a large mixing bowl, cream together the skim milk and sour cream.

2. Fold in the vanilla and mix until it is well blended.

3. Add the cocoa powder and mix completely.

4. Slowly add the icing sugar, a half cup at a time, until it is fully incorporated.

5. Blend until the frosting is smooth.

6. Use the frosting to frost your cupcakes.

Low Fat Cream Cheese Frosting

The final low fat frosting is a twist on the traditional cream cheese frosting. The end result is a light, creamy and extremely tasty frosting without a huge calorie count.

Baking Tips, Tricks and Hints

Before using frozen whipped topping, always warm it up so that it is slightly colder than room temperature. This makes it much easier to use.

Ingredients:

Dry:

- ½ cup of sugar substitute such as Splenda

Wet:

- 1 cup of fat free whipped topping
- 1 cup of fat free cream cheese
- ½ tsp of vanilla

Directions:

1. In a large mixing bowl, cream together the cream cheese and sugar substitute.

2. Add in the vanilla and mix until the icing is creamy.

3. Fold in the whipped cream and mix until it is incorporated. Do not over mix.

4. Use the icing to frost your cupcakes.

Made in the USA
Monee, IL
26 February 2024

54152968R00077